IN THIS MANNER: THEREFORE PRAY

Understanding the Secret
Power of Jesus Christ

Ihemenandu Obasi

authorHOUSE®

AuthorHouse™ UK
1663 Liberty Drive
Bloomington, IN 47403 USA
www.authorhouse.co.uk
Phone: 0800.197.4150

Scripture quotations marked NIV are taken from the Holy Bible, New International Version®. NIV®. Copyright © 1973, 1978, 1984 by International Bible Society. Used by permission of Zondervan. All rights reserved. [Biblica]

Published by AuthorHouse 01/28/2017

ISBN: 978-1-5246-6581-4 (sc)
ISBN: 978-1-5246-6582-1 (hc)
ISBN: 978-1-5246-6580-7 (e)

CONTENTS

Endorsements

This is the testament of a sincere and devout pastor. He points the way forward to communion with Christ through the experience of prayer. He concludes with the power of faith and prayer to change for good not only individuals but the world in general.

Joan Goodall M.A Ed,
London United Kingdom.

In this book, all Christians are being challenged to take prayer as seriously as drinking water. It is our lifeline to God, yet so often our weakness. Through prayer and fasting, we will see God move through our land and our world, bringing changes we thought impossible.

Hilary Taylor,
Small Church Enabler,
London United Kingdom.

This book on prayer in is simplicity form inspires you to want to spent time with God. And with these principles being applied, l only can see us being effective and fruitful in our Christian walk and fellowship with our savior Jesus Christ

Pastor Robert Layman,
Kingdom dynamics chapel,
United Kingdom.

DEDICATION

I want to gratefully dedicate this book to the people who hunger and desire to learn how to pray from our Lord Jesus Christ.

To all my friends and families who stood with me in prayers and encouragements.

To Christ Assembly Christian Church London who gave me the platform to minister the message that gave birth to this book.

To all the people that invested their time and energy to proofread and edit this work.

Thank you and God bless in Jesus Christ Name.

Acknowledgements

I want to personally thank the following persons: Joan Goodall and Kenechukwu Chukwunwejim for working together with me in discussions, researches, proofreading, editing and making this work to become a book. Two of you are God's special angels sent into my life to fulfill my calling in this earth. Thank you very much.

FOREWORD

<u>In This Manner</u> is a book that holistically targeted its content to embrace the totality of prayer principles according to biblical stance. It is a book that is doctrinal unwavering, undiluted, and uncompromising. It is simply written, richly loaded, cleverly illustrated and interestingly packaged for audience from diverse educational strata, denominational standpoint and spiritual mellowness.

The author of this book, Ihemenadu Obasi, ingeniously hinges the book on the "Lord's Prayer." He built the central theme of the book from the Lord's Prayer, elaborating on how to pray. Pastor Ihemenandu, went further to elucidate the efficacy of prayer and fasting bringing in a fresh insight and enlightenment to the mountainous books on prayer and fasting already in circulation. Making the book, <u>In This Manner: Therefore Pray</u> an exceptional, rare, and outstanding piece of non-fiction work and religiously enthused.

<u>In This Manner: Therefore Pray</u> is a book well tailored to meet the need of any true Christian searching for effective and efficient means to communicate with the Infinite Intelligence. The book was spared of the

complexity, perplexity, and superfluous display of theological innuendos that throw readers into a state of trying to make head and tail of a book.

Pastor Ihemenadu Obasi, conscientiously and unreservedly decanted his wealth of knowledge, experience and spiritual encounter with the Holy Spirit in this book. The manner in which Our Lord Jesus Christ taught His disciples how to pray comes into play in this book, as the author step by step throws a greater light on how we Christian should pray, modeling Our Lord's Prayer.

The book also talked about fasting as a means to strengthen our prayer life and to battle against issues and powers stubborn to our prayers. We live in a world not devoid of troubles and challenges, this book unambiguously enumerated how we can sail through this stubborn storm with prayer and fasting.

Many people have been worried by unanswered prayer and lack of breakthrough in life, Pastor Iheme in this book explained the reasons behind such and how to avoid it. Prayer and fasting has a key to open doors permanently closed by Satan, especially when one does it in the manner that was expounded and explicated in the book, <u>In This Manner: Therefore Pray</u>.

KENECHUKWU CHUKWUNWEJIM M.Th, MBA, PGD, HND, PDip.pm.
Resident Pastor, Victory Christian Mission London

CHAPTER 1

The Thirst For Prayer

Texts: Luke 11:1-10; Matthew 6:5-15.

According to the gospel of Luke 11, One day after Jesus Christ finished praying in a certain place; his disciples came and asked Him **'Lord teach us to pray...'** The disciples of Jesus had been watching Him and realized that Almighty Father always answers his prayers and that the secret of his power and humility came through prayer. For this reason, they strongly desired to learn how to pray like Him. One day, after watching Him, one of them quickly asked Him, **'Lord, Teach us to pray.'**

Just like the early disciples of Jesus Christ, today's Christians should strongly desire and hunger to pray. It is important to every Christian to go back to the school of prayer and ask our Lord Jesus Christ to teach us to pray. We should emulate the early disciples to hunger and strongly desire to pray like our master Jesus Christ so that we can achieve the same results in all aspects of life like Him. Prayer is very important to every Christian who wants to grow spiritually in the knowledge and in walk with God.

WHAT IS PRAYER?

According to Andrew Murray, prayer is a key to unlock the doors to a rich, peaceful and joyous life. To pray is to mount on eagle's wings above the clouds and get into the clear heaven where God dwells. It is to enter the treasure house of God and gather riches out of an inexhaustible storehouse (Charles Spurgeon). Prayer is a means of communication between man and God. Prayer enables us to overcome all temptations, doubts, fears, difficulties and dilemmas of life. By prayer we make our needs, problems, worries and concerns known to God. "It is the greatest power God has put into our hands for service" (Mary Slessor). The power lies in prayer when we pour out our heart and spirit to God to receive it.

"I would rather teach one man to pray than ten men to preach" (Charles Spurgeon).

BASIC FUNDAMENTAL TRUTHS ABOUT PRAYER

YOU ARE ALONE WITH GOD (Matthew 6:5-6).

When you come to pray, bear in mind that you are in the presence of God and He is there with you. You are been separated alone with God to seek and commune with Him. It is not an ordinary place but a Holy place. Therefore it is not a place to joke but a place to commune with our Heavenly Father, the God of our Lord Jesus Christ. He is seeing and hearing you and will do whatever He heard you say.

So tell them, "as surely as I live, declares the Lord,
I will do to you the very thing I heard you say.
(Numbers 14:28, NIV).

UNDERSTAND THAT GOD KNOWS YOUR NEEDS.

It is not by how long we spend or by how many words that means we receive answers to our prayer but it is by our faith. God knows our needs even before we start to pray.

When you pray, don't babble on and on as people of other religions do. They think their prayers are answered merely by repeating their words again and again. Don't be like them, for your Father (God) knows exactly what you need even before you ask him!
(Matthew 6:7-8, NLT).

Jesus Christ instructed us to avoid meaningless repetitions of prayers like the pagans do. The people of other religions are known for heaping up empty phrases or babble on and on, for they think their prayers will be answered simply by repeating their words again and again. Do not be like them; God knows exactly what we need even before we pray.

Wording of prayers, quoting scriptures to show you know or well verse in the Bible, use of big grammars or theological jargons in other to impress the people are some of paganism style Christ warned to avoid. It does not matter whether we quote the chapter and the verse in our prayers, what matters is praying with the right word of God. For the God we speak to know the scriptures and the satan we address also knows the scriptures, avoid meaningless repetitions or wrong attitudes.

Many have falling into the temptation of quoting chapter and verses to puff up or show they know better than others thereby expecting everybody to bow to them instead of focusing their mind and prayers to God. Such people have received their rewards by the praise of men.

I remembered one Sunday afternoon travelling to visit a family. As we were in the house, the husband raised an issue of what happened in the church that very morning. He said, "when they go to church, some people will be drawing attention to themselves or behaving as if they are the only one that knows God." All these are pagan styles Christ warned every Christian to avoid.

Moreover some practice it to attract attentions, respect, win trust and prestige of church members and leaders so that they will be recognized as super prayer warriors, whose prayers shake and cause God to bow, but it is not so. God knows your needs even before you pray.

Repetition of prayers shows lack of faith, double mindedness, fear, instability and lack of trust to God. Please understand repetition of prayers is different from persistent prayer. Persistent prayer means never give up on our request to God until it is granted (Luke 18:1). The hallmark of pagan prayers is continual use of vain repetitions thinking that God has not heard their previous request. This is called spiritual babbling of prayers. God's ears are attentive and open to hear us even our silent prayers like Hannah prayed and He answered and gave her a son named Samuel (1 Samuel 1:12-17).

Please note if the Holy Spirit moves you to pray dramatically or grammatically, as long as you are originally led Him, there is nothing wrong with it, but doing it hypocritically in self deceit and self defeat is completely wrong and Christ warned us to avoid such attitudes and prayers.

ASK IN FAITH AND IT WILL BE GIVEN TO YOU.

Truly I tell you, if you have faith as small as a mustard seed, you can say to this mountain, "Move from here to there," and it will move. Nothing will be impossible for you, (Matthew 17:20, NIV).

A lady came to our church during our Friday prayer service on 7th October, 2016, by 7pm. She newly relocated from Scotland to London and was searching for a good church to join. I was in front of the church building when she saw me and walked to me and ask, 'is it a Christian church?' 'Yes,' I replied, 'come in and join us.' She joined us that night and enjoyed a wonderful and lovely time with God. On Sunday 9th October, 2016, she came and requested to the church to pray for her to get a job urgently because her rent would be expiring in few days and she had no money to pay.

The church lifted up the request and asked God to give her a job before next Sunday so that she can testify. On Wednesday 13th October 2016, she called me in the evening shouting with joy '…pastor, pastor, pastor, God gave me the job.' I praised and thanked God with her. Smith Wigglesworth said, "There is something about believing God that will cause Him to pass over a million people to get to you". The prayer of faith is very effective and powerful.

IT IS ONLY IN THE NAME OF JESUS CHRIST GOD AUTHORISED US TO PRAY.

It is only in the name of Jesus Christ we ask and receive from God, not in any other name. Jesus said, **'if you shall ask any thing in my name, I will do it'** (John 14:14, KJV).

Whatsoever you ask God according to His will in the name of Jesus Christ will be given to you. Ask God anything in the name of Jesus Christ and He will give it to you so that your joy may be full. God will honour and answer your prayers when you pray only in the name of Jesus Christ.

Why should we pray only in the name of Jesus Christ?

> **Therefore God exalted Him to the highest place and gave Him the name that is above every name, that at the name of Jesus every knee should bow, in heaven and on earth and under the earth, and every tongue acknowledges that Jesus Christ is Lord, to the glory of God the Father**
>
> **(Phil. 2:9-11, NIV).**

Jesus' name has authority in heaven, earth and hell. Satan knows this name, and bows at the mention of the name of Jesus. He also knows the believers carries authority and power through the name of Jesus Christ. Brethren, understand that we carry power in the name of Jesus Christ, begin to practice it and take authority over the devil in Jesus' Name.

Jesus Christ is highly exalted and placed above every creature by God. It is God that gave Him the name that is above every other name not man. So that when you call the name of Jesus Christ in troubled times and in any issue every power holding you will bow out. Whether in any planet, under the sea, in the earth, or under the earth if you call the name of Jesus Christ in any issue God will answer and rescue you.

.....everyone who calls on the name of the Lord will be saved (Roman 10:13, NIV). It is the name that carries the authority of God for your salvation, deliverance, provision, blessings, healing, security and success in life (Matthew 1:21; Acts 2:21). ·

The name of Jesus Christ is crucial to every believer to possess their glorious inheritance. All the power and authority of Jesus Christ is embedded in His name. God authorized believers to use this name in prayer. **.....very truly I tell you, my Father will give you whatever you ask in my name** (John 16:23, NIV).

ALLOW THE HOLY SPIRIT TO GUIDE YOU.

The bible called the Holy Spirit our advocate, teacher, comforter, councilor, leader, and the Spirit of truth. According to John 14:26, NIV, it says;

> **But the Advocate, the Holy Spirit, whom the Father will send in my name, will teach you all things and will remind you of everything I have said to you.**

The Holy Spirit is our teacher. If we allow Him in our life, he will teach and guide us on what to pray, and how to effectively pray. He will remind us about everything we need to pray. Some time, we may not know what we ought to pray, that is our exact needs. We may be thinking that cookies and chocolates is what we want. But if we depend on the Holy Spirit for guidance, He will teach and remind us of all things we need to pray.

> **In the same way, the Spirit helps us in our weakness. We do not know what we ought to pray for, but the Spirit himself intercedes for us through wordless groans**
>
> **(Romans 8:26, NIV).**

There are sometimes when we may be weak or distracted but the Holy Spirit will come and help our weaknesses. He intercedes for us through speaking in tongues. Speaking in tongues means praying in another language. It can be the language of men or tongue of angels. It is a heavenly language and beyond human comprehension (1 Corinthians 13:1). Sometimes, we may not know what we are saying but we are speaking to God in unknown language under the leading and influence of the Holy Spirit. There are prayers that need to pray in tongues not with known language of men. In such prayers, our spirits are very high to connect with the Holy Spirit especially through worship so that we can pray according to the will of God to overcome the situations facing us. And when we pray according to the will of God, know truly that God will hear and do whatever we ask Him. (Ephesians 6:18; 1 Corinthians 14:2, 14-15).

PRAY WITH THE WORD OF GOD.

The will of God is the word of God. The knowledge of the word of God means the knowledge of the will of God. God's will is His word. The bible is the compilation of the word of God. If you want to know the will of God for any matter study the Bible and ask the Holy Spirit to open your understanding and teach you the word of God.

> **You study the scriptures diligently because you think that in them you have eternal life. These are the very scriptures that testify about me**
>
> **(John 5:39, NIV).**

It is through the knowledge of the scriptures that we know the will of God because the scriptures are pointing and testifying about Jesus Christ. When we pray with the word of God we are praying according to God's will.

By God's divine power He had given us everything we need for a godly life through the knowledge of Christ (2 Peter 1:3-4). The knowledge of the scriptures means the knowledge of Jesus Christ. So, if you know the scriptures you have known the will of God. And everything we need in this life is inside the scriptures. According to Spurgeon, **"the Bible is a book that you can never finish with. It is like a bottomless well; you can always find fresh truth gushing forth from its pages"**. Study them diligently because God has given us great and precious promises inside it, so that we can participate in divine inheritance.

POSTURE OF PRAYER

We can take any posture comfortable to us. In the bible people prayed kneeling, sitting, standing, bowing, lying down, and lifting up their hands and eyes towards heaven. People also prayed beating their breast (Luke 18:13; Matthew 26:39; Ezra 9:5; Nehemiah 9:5; Exodus 34:8; 1 Chronicle 17:16). God is looking at the sincerity of our heart not our posture. We can also pray walking around especially in long prayers.

IN THIS MANNER, THEREFORE PRAY:

> Our Father in heaven,
> Hallowed be your name.
> Your kingdom come.

Your will be done

On Earth as it is in heaven.

Give us this day our daily bread.

And forgive us our debts,

As we forgive our debtors.

And lead us not into temptation,

But deliver us from the evil one.

For Yours is the kingdom and the

Power and the glory forever. Amen.

(Matthew 6:9-13, NKJV).

OUR FATHER IN HEAVEN....

Jesus told us to begin our prayers by addressing God as Our Father in Heaven. In the bible we will find out Jesus personalizing God as **'My Father.'** He also called God, Holy Father, righteous Father, Lord of heaven and earth (John 17:11, 25; Matthew 11:25). Paul one of the apostles of Christ, in his epistles, also referred to God in the same way like Jesus Christ as God our Father, God the Father, the God and Father of our Lord Jesus Christ, (Roman 1:17; Galatians 1:1; Ephesians 1:3).

Understanding and personalizing the God of our Lord Jesus Christ as 'Our Father' in heaven gives us strong confidence and assurance that our prayers are not in vain. It helps us to know that we have a spiritual Father in heaven that cares about our needs and problems.

> **And don't address anyone here on earth as 'Father,'**
> **for only God in heaven is your spiritual Father,**
>
> (Matthew 23:9, NLT).

Please note, the God of our Lord Jesus Christ who live in heaven is 'Our spiritual Father' while our earthly father is our biological father.

Personal knowledge of God as your spiritual Father in heaven gives you full assurance of faith in Him. It will help you to know who you are to God and who He is to you. The knowledge will destroy and clear all forms of doubts, questions and confusions against God in your heart. Personal knowledge of God as our Father in heaven will strengthen our faith, love, and respect for Him. It will bring us into deeper relationship with God as father and son or daughter. Don't be ashamed to call God in heaven 'Your Father' because He is good.

When a child falls short, a good dad will always be on his side comforting and assuring him that it will be better. The Father's words of encouragement and love will strengthen and motivate the child to face tomorrow boldly without fear of uncertainty. This kind of relationship between them is a true measure of love that bonds them together. If some earthly father knows how to show genuine love to their children, how much more shall our heavenly Father show greater love to us.

> **See what great love the Father has lavished on us, that we should be called children of God. And that is what we are**
>
> **(1 John 3:1, NIV).**

Our heavenly Father is a God of love. He has lavished us with great and special love we cannot find elsewhere. When we come to pray, it is a time of lovely relationship with our heavenly Father, to express our friendship and desires to Him.

In Genesis chapter 3, the Garden of Eden was a fellowship center between God, Adam and Eve. At the cool of the day, God came down to commune together with Adam and Eve. It was like a meeting of friends, not as creator and creature, or boss and servants, but as friends. God saw Adam and Eve as His friends to meet together with every evening.

God is always pleased to see us in His presence. Brethren, see him as your best friend when come to pray. He is not a terrifying or aggressive God as some people may think, but a gentle, humble and powerful, who gives rest to our soul.

Acknowledging Him as our heavenly Father is not a religious attribute but a lovely relationship as father and son. He regards us as His beloved children and wants us to see Him as our dearly beloved heavenly Father who cares for us.

This understanding brings us into ultimate intimacy with Him. He is our God, spiritual Father, and best friend. "So let us come boldly to the throne of our gracious God. There we will receive His mercy, and we will find grace to help us when we need it most" (Hebrew 4:16, NLT).

HALLOWED BE YOUR NAME.

This is called adoration. Adoration is the act of paying honour or expressing your deep love and respect to God. It also means the act of worshipping, glorifying, praising, reverencing, magnifying or exalting God. This is the manner our Lord Jesus Christ taught us on how to begin our prayers to God. This manner of prayer helps to deeply appreciate God's personality through singing of psalms, hymns, and other contemporary songs. It can be done by kneeling down, standing up, lying down or any posture in which the Holy Spirit may lead you. God can be praised through any manner by clapping of hands, shouting, and use of different kinds of instruments, and dancing like King David. Let everything that has breath praise the Lord. Praise Him for His mighty acts and for His excellent greatness. Praise God with the use of sounds instruments and dance (Psalms 150).

Oh that men would praise the LORD for His goodness, and for His wonderful works to the children of men

(Psalm 107:15, KJV).

We can also worship in quietness and on our kneels like Nehemiah,

Then I said: "LORD, the God of heaven, the great and awesome God, who keeps

His covenant of love with those who love Him and keep his commandments (Nehemiah 1:5, NIV).

Nehemiah in his prayer worshipped God quietly by expressing to Him how great and awesome He is. He reminded God of His faithfulness to those who love Him and keep His commandments.

Brethren, you can worship, praise, or exalt God in quietness like Nehemiah, what matters to God is, the sincerity of your heart pouring out to Him in deep love and respect.

To Andrew Murray, "each time, before you intercede, be quiet first, and worship God in His glory. Think of what He can do, and how He delights to hear the prayers of His redeemed people. Think of your place and privilege in Christ, and expect great things".

YOUR WILL BE DONE.....

In Christ's manner of prayer, He taught us to pray according to God's will to be done in every issue. There is a will of God in every matter on earth. In our lives, family or career let the will of God be done. The will of God is more perfect, trustful and better than our own will. Our Lord Jesus Christ took three of disciples to mount Olive to pray with them in readiness for His journey to the cross. In his prayers, He said:

> ...'**My Father, if it is possible, may this cup be taken from me. Yet not as I will, but as you will.**' He went away a second time and prayed, '**My Father, if it is not possible for this cup to be taken away unless I drink it, may your will be done.**
> **He went for the third time, and prayed the same**
> **(Matthew 26:36-44).**

Though the road to the cross will be rough, yet Jesus Christ wanted the will of God to be done instead of His own will. Jesus Christ as a man was seeing persecutions by the soldiers, betrayal by Judas Iscariot, denial by His disciples especially Peter, hate, insults, blasphemy and death penalty by Jews. Yet He prayed and said to God, **"My Father, if it is not possible for this cup to be taken away unless I drink it, may your will be done."**

There are cups or assignments that cannot be taken away from you unless you fulfill them just like Jesus. It is written about you; accept it because it is the will of God concerning you. It will be good for you and pleasing to God. However, it may be painful, stressful or financially demanding, permit it to be done. But be confident of this that after sorrows, pains, test, rejections and reproaches follows glory if you allow God's will to be done.

Human wills are foolishness without God. However, everybody have a free will to choose between different possible courses of action. It can be good or bad, but without God it is folly. In Luke 12:16-21, Jesus Christ told us a story about a rich man. He was a farmer by profession. His farm yielded an abundant harvest. He said to himself,

> **"this is what I will do. I will tear down my barns and build bigger ones, and there I will store my surplus grain. And I'll say to myself. 'You have plenty of grain laid up for many years. Take life easy; eat, drink and be merry." But God said to him, "You**

fool. This very night your life will be demanded from you. Then who will get what you have prepared for yourself?"

This rich man was too self centered and selfish that all he was planning and saying was about himself, no regard for God who gave him the wealth or his fellow human beings. The same night God said to him, "You fool". This night your life will be required from you. He died without enjoying his wealth or knew the people that shared his goods. Brethren, it is foolishness to plan without God. Had this rich man knew God in his life, God who knows the ending from the beginning, would have directed him on how to manage his life and wealth better. The will of God is the best for every human being whether in good or bad times. A woman that surrendered her body to a man for the sake of money to solve her body problems is satisfying her personal will not God's will.

A friend told me a story of what happened in old Kent road London, about a man who was fighting to get rid of his wife and marry another woman to obtain a residence permit. Unfortunately to him, as he was passing through in front of church premises, it happened that service was going on and the guest pastor was ministering. The Holy Spirit spoke to the pastor to inform that man passing by, that if he ever throw away his wife and marry another woman, he will suffer hard. Immediately, the pastor sent for him, and gave him the message. He man was broken and felled on the ground, crying and was asking God to have mercy on his foolish plans. This man was a muslim, that day, he gave his life to Christ and repented from his actions.

No matter what we are passing through, human will may seem easy but not the best. God's will is perfect. He is the beginning and the end; let us allow His will to be done.

> **This is the confidence we have in approaching God: that if we ask anything according to His will, He hears us. And if we know that He hears us - whatever we ask - we know that we have what we asked of Him,**
>
> (1John 5:14-15, NIV).

The will of God is the confidence every Christian has to approach God. He hears all our prayers, when we pray according to His will and whatever we ask, we will receive.

...FORGIVE US OUR DEBTS,

This is called Confession. The Greek word for confess is called Omologo. It means to say the same thing and then agree, admit and acknowledge. There is confession of faith, confession of Christ and confession of sin.

In this context, we are looking at confession of sin. Confession of sin means to acknowledge your sin before God.

To some who were confident of their own righteousness and looked down on everyone else, Jesus told this parable: Two men went up to the temple to pray, one a Pharisee and the other a tax Collector. The Pharisee stood by himself and prayed: God, I thank you that I am not like other people - robbers, evil doers, adulterers or even like this tax collector. I fast twice a week and give a tenth of all I get. But the tax collector stood at a distance. He would not even look up to heaven, but beat his breast and said, God, have mercy on me, a sinner. I tell you that this man, rather than the other (Pharisee), went home justified before God. For all those who exalt themselves will be humbled, and those who humbled themselves will be exalted,

(Luke 18:9 - 14, NIV).

Do not come before God like the bragging Pharisee who came to pray before God, 'instead of humbling himself in the presence of God he began to brag to God'. I am not like other people, I am Holier than other people, I am not a robber, I am not an evil doer, I do not commit adultery, like this tax collectors. Instead of focusing his attention to God in humility, he was bragging and boasting to show God how righteous he was.

But the tax collector acknowledged his sins, standing afar off, not able to look up to heaven. And beat his breast as chastisement and prayed to God, **have mercy on me, a sinner.** Jesus said the tax collector went home justified before God instead of the Pharisee. Whenever you come before God humble yourself and confess your sins to Him because there is none righteous, not even one, (Romans 3:10, NIV). Our righteousness is in Christ Jesus not by our might.

> **If we say that we have no sin, we deceive ourselves, and the truth is not in us.**
> **If we confess our sins, he is faithful and just to forgive us our sins, and to cleanse us from all unrighteousness,**
> **(1 John 1:8-9, KJV).**

> **He that covers his sins shall not prosper: but whoso confesses and forsakes them shall have mercy**
> **(Proverbs 28:13, KJV).**

As you come before God in prayer, be transparent and open to Him. Don't cover your sins nor feel that you are too righteous. First forgive anyone that might have sinned against you and then ask God to forgive and have mercy on your own sins. It might be what you did knowingly or unknowingly. Ask Him to remember the blood of Jesus Christ which he shed on the cross for the atonement of your sins and forgive and have mercy on you (Romans 3:25).

THANKSGIVING

There is specific key to every specific door. If you want to enter into the house, you will need to use the right key to open the door. But to enter into the presence of God praises and thanksgiving is the right key that opens the heavenly door.

> **Enter his gates with thanksgiving and his courts with praise; give thanks to Him and praise his name. For the LORD is good and his love endures forever; His faithfulness continues through all generations (Psalm 100:4-5, NIV).**

Enter into the presence of God with praises, worships and thanksgiving because it shows God how you love Him. And you will see how God will speedily answer your prayers.

Before and after you present your supplications or needs to God, give Him thanks for all He has done for you, all that He's doing now and all He's about to do for you. That is, give God thanks for what He has done in the past, what He is doing presently, and what He will do in the future. Praise His name for His love and faithfulness towards you and your family. Do not forget all His benefits and blessings in your life, so give Him thanks.

Give Him thanks for forgiving your sins. Thank Him for your health, protection, provisions, family and other things which you cannot remember (Psalm 103:1-5, NIV).

The book of Luke 17:11-19, told us about the story of ten lepers Jesus healed. Jesus was travelling to Jerusalem, on his way, He met ten lepers and said to them, **"Go show yourselves unto the priests"**. These lepers had not gone far to see the priest and suddenly realized that they were healed. The bible said, one out of the ten, returned with a loud voice glorified God and found Jesus to give Him thanks.

Jesus asked, 'were not all ten cleansed? Where are the other nine? Has no one returned to give praise to God except this foreigner' (Luke 17:17-18, NIV). Jesus requires you to give God praise in anything He does for you. You must return to church or to the person God used to affect the blessings in your life to give thanks for what God has done. If Jesus asked, 'where are the other nine?' that means, God demands your thanksgiving in everything He does for you.

Some people today lack the attitude of appreciation to God let alone their pastor. In their trouble time, they will be looking for God seriously, but when God answers their prayers, they will not return to God again especially to give Him praise. The bible said

….. **thank Him for all He has done**, (Philippians 4:6). Please return to God today and give Him thanks for everything He has done for you because He will keep demanding it from you.

In the book of 2 chronicle 32:25, when Hezekiah the king of Judah, saw that God had delivered him from the hand of Sennacherib king of Assyria and had healed his sicknesses, he became proud and did not thank God appropriately for the kindness shown to him. Brethren, thank God very well and do not allow pride as a manner of some, to deter you from returning to God with praise. Thanksgiving matters so much to God and it is what He requires from you for what He has done.

GIVE US THIS DAY OUR DAILY BREAD….

God seriously is concerned about you. He cares for you. Therefore, tell God all your worries or needs and He will sort you out according to the riches of His glory in Jesus Christ.

Don't worry about anything; instead, pray about everything. Tell God what you need, and thank Him for all He has done,

(Philippians 4:6, NLT).

Give all your worries and cares to God, for He cares about you,

(1Peter 5:7, NLT).

And my God will meet all your needs according to the riches of His glory in Christ Jesus

(Philippians 4:19, NIV).

Please, do not carry those problems alone in the heart, Jesus wants to help and give you rest. Talk to Him now and He will meet all your needs. Remember to thank God afterwards.

There are many people who obtained great results and did mighty things through prayer. These men are:

ELIJAH

He prayed earnestly that it would not rain, and it did not on the land for three and a half years. Again he prayed, and the heavens gave rain, and the earth produced its crops (James 5:17-18).

In another time, Prophet Elijah wanted to turn the hearts of the people of Israel back to the true God, Jehovah. He gathered all the four hundred and fifty prophets of Baal together in the sight of all Israel. He asked the Baal's prophets to call the name of their gods and he would call the name of his own God. The God that answered by fire would be God.

The prophets of Baal took the bullock which was given to them and dressed it. They called the name of their gods from morning till evening but no voice answered them.

At the time of the evening sacrifice, Elijah came and redressed the alter and ordered the people to pour water on it three times until it was flooded. He prayed a simple prayer to Jehovah, the true God, and said;

Answer me, LORD, answer me, so these people will know that you, LORD, are God, and that you are turning their hearts back again. Then fire of the LORD fell and burned up the sacrifice, the wood, the stones and the soil, and also licked up the water in the trench.

When all the people saw this, they fell prostrate and cried, 'The LORD - He is God! The LORD - He is God (1 kings 18:30-39, NIV).

By prayer, Elijah returned the heart of all Israel back to God and they forsook idols and worshipped the living God.

ELISHA

The king of Syria was worried when he understood that the king of Israel always knew all his secret plans. He gathered together all his servants to find out who was the whistle blower among them. One of the servants quickly answered and said, there is none but Elisha the prophet informing the king of Israel whatever he, the king of Syria, had spoken in his bedchamber.

In v.13, he sent spies to find out where Prophet Elisha was. They came back and reported to him that he was in Dothan. The king of Syria quickly sent soldiers with horses and chariots to kidnap him by night. They came and surrounded the whole city of Dothan.

The servant of Elisha got up early in the morning and went out, to behold, an army with horses and chariots had surrounded the city. The servant returned with fear and asked, "my lord, what shall we do?"

'Don't be afraid,' the prophet answered. 'Those who are with us are more than those who are with them.'

And Elisha prayed, 'open his eyes, LORD, so that he may see, 'Then the LORD opened the servant's eyes, and he looked and saw the hills full of horses and chariots of fire all round Elisha. As the enemy came down towards him, Elisha prayed to the LORD, 'strike this army with blindness.' So He struck them with blindness, as Elisha had asked.

Christians, don't be afraid of anything, whatever and whosoever because you are surrounded with angelic army of horses and chariots of fire. Pray and ask God now, **'open my eyes, Oh LORD, so that I may see those that are with me.'**

The servant of Elisha became relaxed and fearless when he saw the horses and chariots of fire round Elisha. Brethren, put this in your heart, God is with you. The enemies will not prevail over your life and destiny. Do not be afraid of anything only pray about them. (2 kings 6:8-20).

HEZEKIAH

The Sennacherib, king of Assyria planned to take the Jews captive because he was not satisfied with the tributes of gold and silver Hezekiah, the king of Judah was paying to him. He sent a large army to take

Jerusalem. The chief commander stood before the walls of Jerusalem, insulted the king of Judah and blasphemed Jehovah their God. Out of ignorance of God and His power, Sennacherib was comparing Him with the gods of the nations he destroyed, saying,

'Did the gods of the nations that were destroyed by my predecessors deliver them - the gods of Gozan, Harran, Rezeph, and the people of Eden.....'

When Hezekiah heard this, he tore his clothes and put on sackcloth and went into the temple of the LORD. He sent Eliakim the palace administrator, shebna the secretary and the leading priests to prophet Isaiah.

Isaiah said to them, 'Tell your master, "This is what the LORD says: do not be afraid of what you have heard - those words with which the underlings of the king of Assyrian have blasphemed me. Listen! When he hears a certain report, I will make him want to return to his own country, and there I will have him cut down with the sword."

While Sennacherib was besieging Lachish, he sent another letter to King Hezekiah boasting to him how powerful he was and ridiculed the living God.

Hezekiah took the letter from his messenger and went up to the temple of the LORD and spread it out before the LORD. He prayed to the LORD, saying:

'LORD, the God of Israel, enthroned between the cherubim, You alone are God over all the kingdoms of the earth. You have made heaven and earth. Give ear, LORD, and hear, open your eyes, LORD, and see; listen to the words Sennacherib Has sent to ridicule the living God. It is true, LORD, that the Assyrian kings have laid waste these nations and their lands. They have thrown their gods into the fire and destroyed them, for they were not gods but only wood and stone, fashioned by human hands. Now, LORD our God, deliver us from his hand, so that all the Kingdoms of the earth may know that you alone, LORD, are God.

That night the angel of the LORD went out and put to death a hundred and eighty - five thousand in the camp of the Assyrian. When the people got up in the next morning, there were all the dead bodies. So Sennacherib broke camp and returned to Nineveh.

One day while he was worshipping in the house of his gods, his sons, Adrammelek and Sharezerkilled killed him (2kings 18:17-37; 19:1-37).

Christians learn to take your needs and problems to God no matter how big and small it may be and He will surely deliver you.

Again, King Hezekiah was very sick to the point of death. Prophet Isaiah came with the word of the LORD to him, saying;

> **Put your house in order, because you are going to die; you will not recover.**

Hezekiah turned his face to the wall and prayed and swept bitterly to the LORD.

The LORD answered, and healed him and added more fifteen years to his life (2Kings 20:1-6). Prayer works if you pray according to the will of God.

DAVID

During the time the Philistines were going to war against the Israelites. David and his men were living in Ziklag, part of the land of the Philistines. He took his men to join the army of Philistines to fight his own people Israel.

The Philistines found the ideal deceitful and reasoned that David and his men could betray them in the heat of the fight and help their people, Israel. Achish, the king of Philistines told David and his men to go.

Then David and his men returned to Ziklag on a three days journey. They saw that the Amalekites had invaded Negev and Ziklag, and destroyed them by fire. They took their wives, sons and daughters and everything else captive. David and his men wept aloud until they had no strength left to weep. The men were so distressed that they were talking to stone David. Everyone was bitter in spirit because of their sons and daughters. **But David encouraged himself in the LORD his God and enquired of Him, and said,**

> **'Shall I pursue after this troop? Will I overtake them? 'Pursue them, 'He (God) answered. 'You will certainly overtake them and succeed in the rescue.'**

Please note, in time of distress avoid argument, blame and disunity. Evil can happen to anyone whether the righteous or the wicked. Hold your peace and take courage from the LORD. Avoid rushing to action and enquire first from God on what next to do.

Make up your mind to obey and take God's advice. And it will be well with you in Jesus Christ name.

It was after David enquired from God on what next to do, he received an assurance that they would recover everything taken from them. And the word from God changed the mind of his men from stoning him. One word of answer from God is powerful enough to avert any despair or danger against your life. Wise men enquire from God before they take action. Seek God first on your plans and allow Him to direct your paths.

THE EGYPTIAN SLAVE.

1. Regarded as a slave but very intelligent.
2. Abandoned to die by his wealthy but foolish master because of hunger, weakness and sickness.
3. For three days, no food and water, no mouthwash, no cream and change of clothes.
4. looked tattered with bad body odour yet a man of blessing and purpose.
5. A foreigner but God's special instrument.

This is the man that held the vital information David and his men needed to succeed in their pursuit. The Amalekite master, as act of foolishness and ignorance threw away the device that held information about him and the entire nation of Amalekite. Be careful who comes and goes in your life. Avoid despising people that come into your life because of race, tribe, colour, rich or poor, gender, young or old. Treat everyone equal.

May be due to pride, fame and prejudice, the rich Amalekite master over looked this sick Egyptian without noting how close he was with him. Because of huge ignorance, the national success was robbed overnight.

Remember, this Egyptian regarded as a slave, hungry, weak and sick held the vital information about the Amalekites national securities, intelligence and treasures but was abandoned on the road to die due to ego and care free attitude. This was an advantage to Amalekites' enemies.

Do you think again and again before you drop people in your life?

Why do you want to part with them?

Are they still useful in your life?

Is it time to say goodbye?

Think again and again. The way you treat people in your life matters a lot. The LORD directs the steps of the godly and delights in every details of their lives (Psalm 37:23, NLT).

God sends people into our life for a reason whether rich or poor, black or white, male or female. Those people were ordained by God from the beginning of the earth to come to us, may be to help us or for we to help them. All things happen for a purpose.

And we know that God causes everything to work together for the good of those who love God and are called according to His purpose for them
(Romans 8:28, NLT).

David's men saw this Egyptian man, who was abandoned to die and brought him to their leader. This man was regarded by the Amalekite as good for nothing but when David saw him, he regarded him as a person who could give them the necessary information about their sons and daughters. Therefore he ordered his men to give him food to eat and water to drink. He ate and was revived.

David with wisdom asked him, **'who do you belong to? Where do you come from?**

Then he revealed himself and the information David and his men desperately needed.

He said, 'I am an Egyptian, the slave of an Amalekite. My master abandoned me when I became ill three days ago. We raided the Negev of the Kerethites, some territory belonging to Judah and the Negev of Caleb. And we burned Ziklag.'

David asked him, 'can you lead me down to this raiding party?'

He answered, 'swear to me before God that you will not kill me or hand me over to my master, and I will take you down to them.'

He led David down, and he fought with them until the evening of the next day and only few escaped. **David recovered everything the Amalekites had taken, including his two wives. Nothing was missing. He brought them back together with flocks and herds of the Amalekites (1 Samuel 30:1-20).**

If you allow God to guide you, not despising whosoever He chooses as an instrument, you will certainly reach your divine destiny and succeed in all your ways.

PETER

When King Herod arrested Apostle Peter and put him in prison. He handed him over to be guarded by four squads of four soldiers each. Herod planned to try him publicly after the Passover.

> **So Peter was kept in prison, but the church was earnestly praying for him**
>
> **(Acts 12:5, NIV).**

The night before King Herod was to bring him to stand for trial, Peter was sleeping between two soldiers, bound with two chains, and guard at the entrance. Suddenly an angel of the Lord appeared and a light shone in the cell. He struck Peter on the side and woke him up.

> **'Quickly, get up!' He said, and the chains fell off Peter's wrists.'**

The angel told him, dress and follow me. Peter followed the angel out of prison.

God will lead you out of every prison and problems you are facing if only you continue in righteousness to put your trust in Him. God will send His angel to release you out of any prison in which satan might have locked you and your family in Jesus Christ name.

You see, heavy satanic or human securities cannot stop God from delivering you, but only unrepentant sin can stop God. The prayer of the upright pleases God (Proverbs 15:8, NIV). If the church can stand in righteousness and earnestly pray, chains, gates, guards will lose their hands because of the power of God. The church will begin to see extraordinary miracles in all aspects of life when they start to pray effectively.

The bible said, **the earnest prayer of a righteous person has great power and produces wonderful results (James 5:16b, NLT).**

God wants to show His power to the world but He is waiting for the church to begin to pray earnestly in righteousness. He wants to set the captives free, heal the sick, raise the dead, touch unyielding sinners to receive salvation, and perform all sorts of wonderful results.

Oh church will you be silent at the time and allow the wonderful works of God to go bye? Arise now in righteousness and begin to pray earnestly like the early church. Nothing will be impossible with God if the church, in one accord, can stand in righteousness and effectively pray for revival and change in the United Kingdom and Europe. Then gates, veils and any high thing standing as an obstacle will give way for the glory of our Lord Jesus Christ to come. But sin hinders God from answering our prayers. The bible said,

> **If I regard iniquity in my heart, the LORD will not hear me**
>
> **(Psalm 66:18, KJV).**

Are you still indulging in sin, whether in secret or open, sin will give you a bad image before God. It will cause God to turn His face and over look your prayers. Repent now and reconcile to God. Confess and forsake them and do not return to those sins again.

He that covers his sins shall not prosper: but whoever confesses and forsakes them shall have mercy
(Proverb 28:13, NKJV).

PAUL AND SILAS

These men were beaten and thrown into prison because Paul rebuked the demon inside a slave girl. And at midnight Paul and Silas prayed and sang praises unto God and other prisoners heard them. God answered their prayers and sent an earthquake that shook the foundations of the prison, opened all doors, and loosed the chains in the hands of every prisoner. Prayer causes God to do mighty works. Just like Paul and Silas, present all your problems or needs to God and He will answer you (Acts 16:16-33).

JOHN KNOX

This is a man known for his prayer **"Give me Scotland, or I die"**. Knox's prayer was not an arrogant demand, but the passionate plea of a man willing to die for the sake of the pure preaching of the gospel and the salvation of his countrymen. God heard his prayers and changed the nation of Scotland to Christ. It was an effective and powerful prayer of a righteous man.

Chapter 2

Hindrances To Answers Prayer

UNFORGIVENESS

And when you stand praying, if you hold anything against anyone, forgive them, so that your Father in heaven may forgive you your sins (Mark 11:25, NIV).

Forgiveness is a prerequisite to every Christian that comes before God to pray. Forgive those that offended you so that your Heavenly Father will also forgive your own sins and answer your prayers. That means God is ready to forgive your sins if you can forgive those that offended you.

> **But if you do not forgive others their sins, your Father will not forgive your sins**
>
> **(Matthew 6:15, NIV).**

Your prayers will not be answered by God when you do not forgive others. Forgiveness paves the way to your prayers to be answered. But lack of forgiveness hinders God from answering your prayers. Therefore, when you stand to pray, first forgive others that offended you, then God will forgive your own sins and answer your prayers.

SIN

Where sin is present a wall has been built between God and man so that there are no means of intercourse between them. Sin is a great barrier between God and man. **Psalms 66:18, (NET), says;**

> **If I had harboured sin in my heart, the Lord would not have listened.**
> **If I regard iniquity in my heart, the Lord will not hear me**
>
> **(Psalms 66:18, KJV).**

Sins in the heart hinder your prayers. Get rid of them because God hates sin.

He will not listen to your prayers if you harbour it in your heart.

Surely the arm of the Lord is not too short to save, nor his ear too dull to hear. But your iniquities have separated you from your God; your sins have hidden his face from you, so that he will not hear

(Isaiah 59:1-2, NIV).

Our God is mighty to save. His ears are wide to hear. He watches all the planets. It is only sins that hinder our prayers and turn His face from us. The eyes of the Lord are too pure to behold evil, and He cannot look on iniquity (Habakkuk 1:13). All those secret sins hinder God from answering your prayer. Let's not deceive ourselves thinking it does not matter.

He that covers his sins shall not prosper: But whosoever confesses and forsakes them shall have mercy

(Proverbs 28:13, NKJV).

Confess all your sins to God both hidden and open sins so that you will receive mercy from God and prosper. Why are we blocking the face of God in our life because of pleasures of the world that do not satisfy nor give rest or peace of mind? Why? God wants you to repent and return back to him now. He would like to show you mercy and prosper you. Humble yourself before Him now and confess all those sins in your heart to Him now.

If we confess our sins, He is faithful and just and will forgive us our sins and purify us from all unrighteousness

(1John 1:9, NIV).

God is very faithful and just to us. When we confess all our sins to Him, He will forgive us and cleanse us from all unrighteousness. As long as you walk in the light, all your sins are cleansed from the very time you confess them. Therefore confess your sins to God when you stand to pray. Do not cover your sins from God because you cannot hide them from Him. Confess them so that He will show mercy and prosper you in all your ways.

Please write this in your heart as a believer;

Nevertheless the foundation of God stands sure, having this seal,
The Lord knows them that are His. And, Let everyone that names the name of Christ depart from iniquity
(2 Timothy 2:19, NKJV).

SATAN

The plan of satan is to stop believers from praying to God. He will try everything to weaken, frustrate, hinder and distract people from prayer.

The Bible called him the archenemy, devil, accuser of the brethren and the deceiver.

> **.....Do not be afraid, Daniel. Since the first day that you set your mind to gain understanding and to humble yourself before your God, your words were heard, and I have come in response to them. But the prince of the Persian Kingdom resisted me twenty - one days. Then Michael, one of the chief princes, came to help me, because I was detained there with the king of Persia**
>
> **(Daniel 10:12-13, NIV).**

I don't know how long satan has been detaining or delaying your prayers, the bible says, resist him in faith and he will flee away from you (1Peter 5:8-9).

"Get out of here, satan," Jesus told him (satan). Then the devil left Him, and angels came and took care of Jesus (Matthew 4:10-11).

Every Christian should understand that satan will not leave you alone until you stand in faith and command him to get out of your life, destiny, family, ministry and business in Jesus Christ name. As a Christian, you must know how to address satan, if not he will keep on detaining your destiny or prayers (Matthew 16:23).

And when he had called unto him his twelve disciples,
He gave them power against unclean spirits, to cast
them out, and to heal all manner of diseases

 (Matthew 10:1, KJV).

God has already given you power from the time you received and believed in Jesus Christ as the son of God and your Lord and Saviour. Make use of the power Christ has given to you to stop satanic oppression and harassment in your life. Remind satan that you overcame him by the blood of the lamb, and by the word of your testimonies (Revelation 12:10-11).

Where your faith is weak and you are finding it difficult to rebuke the devil from your life, cry out in desperation to your saviour Jesus Christ to save you. Ask Him to have mercy on you and save you now from every satanic manipulation and oppression. Read these scriptures and pray with them;

 And everyone who calls on the name of the Lord
 will be saved

 (Acts 2:21, NIV).

 ......and you are to give him the name Jesus, because
 he will save his people from their sins

 (Matthew 1:21, NIV).

The mission of Jesus Christ in your life is to save you from sin or satanic oppressions. Call the name of Jesus Christ loudly and cry to him to save now and He will hear and answer you. God bless you in Jesus Christ name.

WRONG MOTIVES

When you ask, you do not receive; because you ask with wrong motives, that you may spend what you get on your pleasures (James 4:3, NIV).

Sexual immorality, impurity, and debauchery, idolatry, witchcraft, hatred, discord, jealousy, fits of rage, selfish ambition, dissensions, factions and envy, drunkenness, orgies, pornography, are examples of wrong motives or the desires of the flesh. All these hinder God from answering your prayers. Those who live like this will not inherit the kingdom of God (Galatians 5:16-21).

The mind controlled by the things of the flesh does not obey God. Such mind is in enemity with God. And those who live in the flesh cannot please God. Their prayers are hindered because of wrong motives. Check your mind very well before you pray. The purpose of your prayer is it for right motive or for wrong motive? God will not answer if the prayer is for wrong motive. Allow the Holy Spirit to lead you and pray with right motives.

DISUNITY

The bible called it the act of the flesh in Galatians 5:19. Disunity does not please God. Whether in the family, church, business or nations, disunity hinders the answer of your prayers.

> **Again, truly I tell you that if two of you on earth agree about anything they ask for, it will be done for them by my Father in heaven**
>
> **(Matthew 18:19, NIV).**

Husband, whatever you and your wife will agree to and ask God in the name of Jesus Christ, He will answer and do it. But where there is no unity, the prayers are not answered. Unity opens door and speeds up your request to God. Make peace with one and another and be united together. God is not in your midst when there is no unity among you.

> **.....Every kingdom divided against itself will be ruined, and every city or household divided against itself will not stand**
>
> **(Matthew 12:25, NIV).**

No nation, Kingdom, church and family can stand without unity. Unity is the back bone that upholds family, organization, Kingdom and churches together. Without unity you cannot stand and your prayers will not be answered by God.

DOUBT

In biblical context, doubt is an attitude or feeling of uncertainty or lack of conviction of the word or promises of God. According to the king James Dictionary, doubt means to waver or fluctuate in opinion. It is also a fluctuation of mind respecting truth or propriety, arising from defect of knowledge or evidence.

> **But when you ask, you must believe and not doubt, because the one who doubts is like a wave of the sea, blown and tossed by the wind.**
> **That person should not expect to receive anything from the Lord.**
> **Such a person is double - minded and unstable in all they do.**
>
> **(James 1:6-8, NIV)**

The bible says, a man who doubts is an unstable man. He lacks enough faith to claim or lay hold of the promises of God for his life. Doubt or unbelief is a sin against God.

And without faith it is impossible to please God, because anyone who comes to Him must believe that He exists and that He rewards those who earnestly seek Him

(Hebrews 11:6, NIV).

Doubt does not please God and it hinders answers to prayer. Those who doubt question the existence, faithfulness, power, character and goodness of God. The bible says, the person who doubts is like a wave of the sea, blown and tossed by the wind. That person should not expect to receive anything from the Lord.

Stop doubting God from now and pray thus:

Oh God, help me overcome my doubts so that I can believe in You in Jesus Christ name

(Mark 9:24, NIV).

WORRIES

This is a state of thinking about problems or fears. It also means the state of being anxious and troubled over actual or potential problems. Jesus warned us against worries, and said, **"Do not let your hearts be troubled** .....(John14:1, NIV). As a Christian, God does not want you to be worried. Worry damages both your spiritual and physical well being. It is a subtle weapon Satan uses to frustrate people's prayer. **"The devil knows if he can capture your thought life he has won a mighty victory over you"** (Smith Wigglesworth). Our Lord and saviour Jesus Christ told us a parable in Matthew 13: 3-4,7, 22, NIV, and said;

A farmer went out to sow his seed. As he was scattering the seed, some fell along the path, and the birds came and ate it up.

Other seed fell among thorns, which grew up and choked the plants.

In verse 22, He explained about the thorns.

> **The seed falling among the thorns refers to someone who hears the word, but the worries of this life and the deceitfulness of wealth choke the word, making it unfruitful.**

Jesus described worries of life as thorns that destroy the word of God and make it unfruitful. And anything that destroys the word of God in your heart will steal your joy and happiness. If the word of God is destroyed or made unfruitful, that Christian cannot pray. Worries of life render Christians prayerlessness. It choked, crushed and dried their spiritual life so that they will be unable to pray. The bible says;

Do not be anxious about anything, but in every situation, by prayer and petition, with thanksgiving, present your requests to God

(Philippians 4:6, NIV).

God want us to bring all of our needs and problems to Him in prayer instead of worrying about them. In Matthew 6:25-34, Our Lord Jesus admonishes us to avoid worrying about our physical needs but seek first the kingdom of God and His righteousness, and all our needs will be given to us by Him. That means, there is no need to worry about anything rather present them to God in prayer and He will supply you all your needs according to His glorious riches in Christ Jesus (Philippians 6:19).

Cast all your anxiety on Him because He cares for you

(1Peter 5:7, NIV).

The plan of God concerning our problems is not to leave us alone with it. He wants us to bring all our worries and concerns to Him because He cares for us. No matter how big, small or difficult the problems look like, there is nothing too hard for God to do. With God all things are possible. Bring all your worries and concerns to God and He will give rest.

For those who have not received Christ into their life as Lord and saviour, Jesus Christ still wants them to bring all their problems to Him. He said to them:

Come to me, all you who are weary and burdened, and I will give you rest. Take my yoke upon you and learn from me, I am gentle and humble in heart, and you will find rest for your souls.
For my yoke is easy and my burden is light

(Matthew 11:28:30, NIV).

No matter your colour, race, gender, nationality, rich or poor, Jesus Christ invites you now to bring all your problems to Him and He will give the peace of mind you want.

He does not want you to be carrying those heavy burdens around. He wants you to bring them to Him and find rest to your soul. But this will be a good opportunity for you to receive Jesus Christ into your life. If you don't mind, say this simply pray:

Dear Heavenly Father,
I come to You in the Name of Jesus Christ.
Your word says, "....he that comes to me I will in no wise cast out"
(John 6:37), so I know You won't cast me out, but You take me in and I thank You for it.

You said in Your word, "whosoever shall call upon the name of the Lord shall be saved"

(Rom. 10:13). I am calling on Your Name, so I know You have saved me now.

You also said ".... If you confess with your mouth the Lord Jesus and believe in your heart that God has raised Him from the dead, you will be saved.

For with the heart one believes unto righteousness, and with the mouth confession is made unto salvation (Romans 10:9-10, NKJV). I believe in my heart now Jesus Christ is the Son of God. I believe that He was raised from the dead for my justification, and I confess Him now as my Lord.

Because Your word says, "..... With the heart man believes unto righteousness...." and I do believe now with my heart, I have now become the righteousness of God in Christ (2 Cor. 5:21). .... And I am saved! Thank You, Lord Jesus Christ!

PRIDE

God looks at the heart not at the outward appearance or what we think that we are. The Pharisee forgot to understand that when you come to God you must humble yourself because He searches the heart and the secret motives of anyone that comes to Him to reward them. He was too full of self confidence of his righteousness and proud of his self achievements to God that he went home not justified. God turned His face away from him and did not answer his prayers. But the tax collector came and humbled himself before God. Acknowledge his sins and ask for mercy. Jesus said, this humble man went home justified before God rather than the Pharisee.

For all those who exalt themselves will be humbled, and those who humble themselves will be exalted (Luke 18:14b, NIV).

Do not be like the proud Pharisee, for our faithfulness is by the grace of God. If you are beautiful or handsome it is because of the grace of God (1 Corinthians 4:7). Your achievements, position and fame are all given to you by God through His grace. You received everything you have from God not by your might (1 Corinthians 4:7). For this reason, do not allow pride enter into your heart.

Let nothing puff you up because God opposes the proud and shows favour to the humble. Younger people should submit themselves to the elder people. Everybody should put on humility as clothes. "Humble yourselves, therefore, under God's mighty hand, that He may lift you up in due time." (1 Peter 5:5-6). It is through humility that you can find favor from God but pride will turn God's face away from you.

LAZINESS

This is another subtle hindrance to prayer. Laziness is the quality of being unwilling to work or use energy. Some Christians lack the willingness to get up and pray especially early in the morning. They love to sleep or do any other activities more than to pray even an hour.

> **Then He returned to His disciples and found them sleeping. 'Couldn't you men keep watch with me for one hour?' He asked Peter. 'Watch and pray so that you will not fall into temptation. The spirit is willing, but the flesh is weak.'**
>
> **(Matthew 26:40-41, NIV).**

We are living in an era of modern technology and fast growing social media such as face book, Instagram, LinkedIn, Yahoo Messenger, what's app, Email, imo, Deezer, Hangouts, etc. Many Christian spend a lot of time on social media than in prayer. They waste their time on video calls, movies and messages, and end up too weak to pray. Please, it is important to understand that the use of social medias or modern technologies are not sin on their own but lack of discipline on them is likely to lead to prayerlessness.

Peter, James, and John couldn't wait and pray even for one hour because their body was too weak. Brethren, when you spend all the time on social media, movies, and video calls, in the night, you will definitely become weak and have no time to pray. Even when it is necessary or not necessary, discipline yourself and schedule time for everything.

Some spend all night drinking and partying with friends and give no time to prayer. All these things hinder prayer.

CONTROL YOURSELF IN EVERYTHING.

But I discipline my body and keep it under control, lest after preaching to others I myself should be disqualified (1Corinthians 9:27, ESV).

The Bible says discipline your body because you still have the nature of flesh. It is your spirit that is born again not your body. Your body will want to keep on doing the things it used to do or want to do. But discipline your body and keep it under your control.

Lack of self control destroys destiny and life. Paul says: ....lest after preaching to others, I myself should be disqualified. Do you know that laziness can disqualify you from God? It is able to hinder the blessings, promises and God's plans for your life.

Discipline yourself and begin now to manage your time well in everything that you do especially in your prayer life.

Chapter 3

Forgiveness

Forgive us our sins, for we also forgive everyone who sins against us (Luke 11:4, NIV).

> **For if you forgive other people when they sin against you, your Heavenly Father (God) will also forgive you. But if you do not forgive others their sins, your Father (God) will not forgive your sins**
> **(Matthew 6:14-15, NIV).**

Forgive means to pardon, or to cancel a debt. It is a requirement or condition you must meet for God to answer your prayers. Forgiveness could be giving up your right to hurt someone for hunting you. It is a decision to let go of resentment and thoughts of revenge.

It is impossible to live in this dangerous, corrupt and fragile world without being abused, harmed, offended, challenged, rejected, misunderstood, defrauded, cheated, hated or deceived. Learning to respond properly is the key basics of Christian living.

If you hurt or wrong someone, seek for forgiveness in order to restore the relationship. If nation "A" wrongs nation B, that nation "A" should seek for forgiveness from nation "B" to restore their relationship for the peace, progress, prosperity, and security of the world. And nation B must accept the forgiveness so that God will forgive their sins. If Mr K wrong Mr Z, Mr k should seek for forgiveness for the peace, unity, progress and security of each other. And Mr Z must forgive so that God will also forgive him his own sins. Do not harden your heart nor pretend that you have forgiven when you have not done so in your heart. Be sincere and forgive just as you would want God to forgive you. Do not forgive because the person deserves or merits to be forgiven. Rather forgive as you would like God to do to you. Forgive with love, mercy and grace. However, we need to watch our actions to avoid falling into bad behaviours. Forgiving others means to release from your heart the wrong they did to you. This brings a special inner peace of mind that enables you to move on with life. If you chose not to release and forgive them, God, your Heavenly Father, will not forgive your own sins or wrongs.

For everyone has sinned; we all fall short of God's glorious standard.

(Romans 3:23, NIV).

Again, remember, no one is perfect. It is necessary to forgive because one day you may need another person to forgive you too.

THE BENEFITS OF FORGIVENESS

Forgiveness is the key that opens door for God to answer your prayers.

> **For if you forgive other people when they sin against you, your Heavenly Father will also forgive you. But if you do not forgive others their sins, your Heavenly Father will not forgive your sins**
> **(Matthew 6:14-15, NIV).**

Unforgiveness separate us from God. It is a sin. It does not allow God to answer our prayers. It opens the door to bitterness, resentments, stress, anxiety, hatred, witchcraft, disunity, jealousy, anger, selfish ambition, division, envy, depression, mental affliction, frustration and gives satan the chance to enter to steal, kill and destroy lives, while forgiveness closes these evil doors.

Take this advice from Proverbs 24:29, NIV.

> **Do not say, I'll do to them as they have done to me. I'll pay them back for what they did.**

The Bible said, never say that you will revenge, instead forgive them so that God will also forgive you your own sins, no matter what they did to you.

Forgiveness sets you free and carries away the heavy burdens from your heart. It is good for you because if you chose not to forgive, you will continue to feel hurt, disappointed, depressed and be carrying unnecessary burden on your heart. Therefore, forgive in order to release yourself and others from the agony of bondage, because it is a means to freedom. **So Christ has truly set us free. Now make sure that you stay free... (Galatians 5:1, NLT).**

Forgiveness brings progress and helps you to be productive in life. As soon as you release and forgive, someone that hurts you, peace, love, joy, grace will begin to flow in your heart. Unity and progress and prosperity will begin immediately. Within a short period of time you will realize some extraordinary changes in all aspects of your life.

But unforgiveness hinders progress, peace, unity, prosperity and builds a wall of separation from each other. Forgiveness moves you forward and restores to you all that satan has taken from you.

Get rid of all bitterness, rage and anger, brawling and slander, along with every form of malice. Be

kind and compassionate to one another, forgiving each other, just as in Christ God forgave you.

(Ephesians 4:31-32, NIV).

The earlier you get rid of unforgiveness in your heart and forgive just like Jesus Christ forgave you, the better for you.

Forgiveness brings healing whether physically, spiritually, mentally, financially, and in all aspects of life. Forgiveness destroys bitterness and resentments and unites families, ministries, businesses and nations together.

If my people, who are called by my name, will humble themselves and pray and seek my face and turn from their wicked ways, then I will hear from heaven, and I will forgive their sin and will heal their land (1 Chronicle 7:14, NIV).

But I want you to know that the son of Man has authority on earth to forgive sins. So he said to the paralyzed man, 'Get up', take your mat and go home

(Matthew 9:6, NIV).

This man has been paralyzed for thirty eight years. But it was when Jesus Christ forgave his sins that he was healed.

Forgiveness brings healing to broken relationships, reduces stress, worries, blood pressure, depression, and hostility. It leads to a stronger immune system, improved healthier heart and increases self esteem. According to 2011 study in the journal of Behavioural medicine, people who practice conditional forgiveness - in other words, people who can only forgive if others say sorry first or promise not to do the transgression again - may be more likely to die earlier, compared with people who are less likely to practice conditional forgiveness. So forgive as quickly as possible.

FORGIVENESS IS ALWAYS.

Then Peter came to Jesus and asked, **"LORD, how many times shall I forgive my brother or sister who sins against me? Upto seven times? Jesus answered, "I tell you, not seven times, but seventy - seven times".** (Matthew 18:21-22, NIV).

What Jesus means is that there is no number of times your brother or sister will sin against you and you refuse to forgive him or her. But wisdom should teach us to forgive and avoid putting ourselves into his or her behavioural risk if the person still opposes a risk to our lives.

FORGIVENESS MAKES US PURE.

If we confess our sins, He (God) is faithful and just and will forgive us our sins and purify us from all unrighteousness (1John 1:9, NIV).

Forgiveness brings purity from God. Through forgiveness, God purifies us from all unrighteousness and makes us a special instrument for special purpose, made Holy and fit, useful and prepared to do any good work for Jesus Christ.

FORGIVENESS IS STRENGTH.

According to the Oxford dictionary, strength means the quality or state of being physically strong. To forgive does not mean that you are weak as some people may think. Mahatma Gandhi said, **"Forgiveness is the virtue of the brave"**. You are a strong person when you are able to release and forgive someone. You have taken the grace of God to release yourself from the effects of that sin, such as bitterness, grudges and opens new door for God to handle the situation by Himself (2 Thessalonians 1:6, NIV). It also shows that you are an obedient child of God when you take strength and forgive anyone that hurts you.

And when you stand praying, if you hold anything against anyone, forgive them, so that your Father (God) in heaven may forgive you your sins

(Mark 11:25, NIV).

There are men of great characters who forgave even when the evil committed against them looks unpardonable. These are:

JOSEPH

The story of Joseph and his brothers is written in the book of Genesis. It counts the evil deed committed against him by his family members and how he forgave them at the end.

Joseph was one of the twelve sons of Jacob. He was hated by his brothers because of his dreams and special love his father had for him. Joseph and his brothers were shepherds. His father, one day sent him to go and see how his brothers and the flocks were faring in the field. Unfortunately for him, when he came to his brothers in the field, they over powered him and pulled off his clothe of many colours which his father had made for him due to the special love he had for him, and threw him into a dried pit, and they later sold him into slavery to the Ishmaelite merchants travelling to Egypt. The Ishmaelite took him to Egypt and sold him to Potiphar, an officer of Pharaoh and captain of the guard. The LORD was with Joseph, he found favour before him. Potiphar made him his personal assistant and placed him in charge of everything in his house.

Joseph got into problems with Potiphar's wife because she wanted him to sleep with her. When Joseph refused to sleep with her, she accused him of trying to rape her. This accusation provoked Potiphar and he sent Joseph to prison.

But the LORD was with Joseph, and showed him mercy, and gave him favour in the sight of the chief prison officer, and because of this, the chief prison officer placed him in charge of other prisoners and whatsoever he did, the LORD made it prosper.

After some times, the butler and the baker of Pharaoh, the king of Egypt, offended their lord Pharaoh. The king was very wroth against them. He sent them to prison where Joseph was.

They had a dream one morning and were confused about the dream. Joseph came in to see them in the morning, and saw that they were sad. He asked them why are you sad? The Pharaoh's officers told him about their dreams and Joseph gave interpretations of the dreams. After three days, the dreams were fulfilled as Joseph interpreted it. While the butler was about to leave, Joseph asked him to tell Pharaoh about him so that he could release him but the butler forgot him.

After two years, Pharaoh, the king of Egypt, had disturbing dreams that even his magicians could not interpret. The butler remembered Joseph and told Pharaoh about him. Pharaoh sent for Joseph. The king's officers quickly brought Joseph out of prison, shaved and clothed him properly to go before Pharaoh.

Joseph listened to the dreams of Pharaoh. He interpreted the dreams and advised him wisely on what to do. Pharaoh was so pleased with Joseph that he made him his second in command.

When the famine began, so many nations including Canaan were touched and Egypt was the only country that had food.

Jacob sent his ten sons to Egypt to buy food. When Joseph's brothers got to Egypt, they did not recognize Joseph when they saw him. They bowed to their Joseph, who recognized them and did not reveal himself to them. He remembered the dreams which he dreamt of them. He spoke very harshly and accused them of spying in Egypt. While his brothers were trying to defend themselves revealed whom they were and about their youngest brother Benjamin.

In summary, He later released them and asked them to go and bring the entire family to Egypt. Joseph's brothers got home and told Jacob their father about the news. Jacob did not believe them at the very first time, but when he saw the gifts from Joseph, he agreed.

They came to Egypt with the entire family and livestock and settled in Goshen.

Jacob was one hundred and thirty years old when he came to Egypt. He died after seventeen years in Egypt. Joseph's brothers were afraid of revenge for the evil they committed against Joseph when their father was sick. Jacob before he died asked Joseph to forgive his brothers. His brothers even offered to give themselves to become his servants. But Joseph rejected the offer because it was completely not important to him for he had proved his love to them in many ways. He said to them,

> **'Don't be afraid. Am I in the place of God? You intended to harm me, but God intended it for good to accomplish what is now being done, the saving of many lives. .....don't be afraid. I will provide for you and your children.**
>
> (Genesis 37;39-50).

Joseph reassured them of their security and spoke kindly to them even though he was in a high position to repay them their evil deed, but chose to forgive.

JESUS CHRIST, OUR EXAMPLE

Jesus Christ was betrayed by one of his closest disciples named Judas Iscariot. He was the financial treasurer of the ministry of Christ. During the feast of Passover, chief priests and teachers of the law were looking for some way to kill Jesus. Judas Iscariot, one of the twelve disciples, went and conspired with them on how he might betray his master Jesus. They were delighted and agreed to pay him money. As Jesus was coming down from mount Olives, where he went with three of his disciples to pray, Judas Iscariot came with chief priests, the officers of the temple guard, and elders and betrayed his master with a kiss. But Jesus asked him, 'Judas, are you betraying the son of man with a kiss?' Even with this warning, Judas Iscariot without remorse went ahead and betrayed Jesus because of the love of money.

They arrested Jesus and took him to the house of the chief priest, but Peter, one of the twelve disciples, who promised and said, 'Lord, I am ready to go with you to prison and death,' was following at a distance due to fear. He was supposed to be on his master's side but was following him at a distance. Peter publicly denied Jesus three times within a few hours because of fear.

In the house of the chief priest, Jesus was beaten, mocked, blindfolded and insulted. The Jews falsely accused him before Pilate. But after trial, Pilate found no fault in Him. Then he sent him to Herod.

In the house of Herod, the soldiers ridiculed and mocked him. He then sent him back to Pilate because he found no fault in Jesus. For the sake of Jesus trials, the conflict between Pilate and Herod was settled and they became friends again.

Pilate called together the chief priests, the rulers and the people, and said to them, 'You brought me this man as one who was inciting the people to rebellion. I have examined him in your presence and found no basis for your charges against him. Neither has Herod, for he sent him back to us; as you can see, he has done nothing to deserve death' (Luke 23:13-15, NIV).

Yet the Jews shouted to Pilate, **"Crucify him, crucify him"**.

Three times, Pilate tried to convince the Jews that Jesus did nothing to deserve death. The Jews because of their stubborn attitudes and hate refused to listen to Pilate but wanted him to be killed. When Pilate saw he could not change their mind, he decided to grant their demand, and handed Jesus over to them to be killed.

They led him to the place of the skull, called Golgotha in the Hebrew language. They crucified him along with two criminals, one on his right and the other on his left.

Jesus, instead of cursing his disciples for leaving him alone when he needed them most or pronouncing curse on Judas Iscariot for betraying him for the sake of money or the Jews for crucifying him on the cross, He prayed to God to forgive them and said:

'Father, forgive them, for they do not know what they are doing'

(Luke 23:34).

This is a good example of forgiveness for every Christian to follow.

I will recommend you to watch the film: Passion for Christ, so that you can understand how Christ suffered for your sake and later forgave all his enemies.

STEPHEN

Stephen was the first Christian martyr. While he was preaching the good news of Jesus Christ, at a point, he rebuked the Jews of their sins. The members of the Sanhedrin heard this, and became furious at him. They rushed at him, and dragged him out of the city and began to stone him. Stoning to death was a capital punishment characterized with shame and injuring during the Roman era.

While they were stoning him, Stephen prayed, **'Lord Jesus, receive my spirit.' Then he fell on his knees and cried out, 'Lord, do not hold**

this sin against them.' When he had said this, he fell asleep (Acts 7:59-60, NIV).

Emulate Stephen and do not carry grudges, bitterness, hatred, and resentment to the grave. As long as you are alive, forgive them that hurt you because there is no chance of forgiveness in the grave. Do not hold any sin against anyone; forgive as you will want God to forgive your sins.

NELSON MANDELA

Mandela was the first black president of South Africa from 1994 - 1999, elected under democratic election. He was a freedom fighter, anti-apartheid advocate, an African nationalist, Philanthropist and politician.

In 1962, he was arrested by the apartheid government accusing him of conspiring to overthrow the state and sentenced to life imprisonment. He was imprisoned for 27years serving in three prisons such as Robben Island, Pollsmoor Prison and Victor Verster prison.

President F. W. de Klerk released him in 1990 because of the international pressures and increasing fear of a racial civil war. Mandela and de Klerk worked out an end to apartheid and organized the 1994 multiracial general election in which Mandela led the African National Congress (ANC) to victory and became the president.

He made F. W. de KLerk, who was one of the enemies of blacks, his second deputy and said:

> **To make peace with an enemy, one must work with that enemy, and that enemy becomes your partner.**

On his first public address to the black majorities after the election result, he said;

> **"Free at last! Free at last! I stand before you humbled by your courage, with a heart full of love for all of you. I regard it as the highest honour to lead the ANC at this moment in our history. I am your servant.... It is not the individuals that matter, but the collective.... This is a time to heal the old wounds and build a new South Africa."**

Mandela saw the victory as a mission of peace, reconciliation, building trust, confidence and healing the wounds of the South African not an opportunity to revenge the white minorities for their evils. There was a big feeling of anxiousness among the White and other minorities about their future. He assured them to feel secure that the freedom was not a fight against any one group or colour, but a battle against a system of repression. Mandela encouraged unity and forgiveness between the black majorities and the white minorities to join hands with one another for a better country and declared South Africa **one country, one nation, one people, marching together into the future.**

Forgiveness is the best answer to peace not revenge or war. The greatest history you can make is to make peace with one another irrespective of race, colour or gender.

Mahatma Gandhi said; **"An eye for an eye only ends up making the world blind."**

Do not think about revenge but think of forgiveness and peace with each other.

CHAPTER 4

The Power of Fasting and Prayer

When they came to the crowd, a man approached Jesus and knelt before him.

"Lord, have mercy on my son, he said. He has seizures and is suffering greatly. He often falls into the fire or into the water. I brought him to your disciples, but they could not heal him. 'You unbelieving and perverse generation,' Jesus replied, 'how long shall I stay with you? How long shall I put up with you? Bring the boy here to me.'

Jesus rebuked the demon, and it came out of the boy, and he was healed at that moment. Then the disciples came to Jesus in private and asked, 'why couldn't we drive it out?' He replied, because you have so little faith. Truly I tell you, if you have faith as small as a mustard seed, you can say to this mountain, move from here to there, and it will move. Nothing will be impossible for you" (Matthew 17:14-20, NIV).

"However, this kind does not go out except by prayer and fasting"

(Matthew 17:21, NKJV).

The disciples of Jesus received their highest rebuke and disgrace due to lack of faith to heal the sick boy. Even the father of the sick boy was frustrated with the inability of the disciples to drive out the little demon from his son. When he saw their master Jesus Christ coming down from the mountain of prayer with some of His disciples, he ran to Him and knelt before Him. And said, Lord, have mercy on my son, he has seizures and is suffering greatly. He often falls into the fire or into the water. I brought him to your disciples, but they could not heal him.

Jesus was very angry with his disciples because He had taught them so many things about the kingdom and has been with them one by one so that they can learn and have enough faith in Him. Because of their unbelief Jesus rebuked them and said, **O faithless and perverse generation, how long shall I be with you? How long shall I suffer you? Bring him hither to me.** Please understand these things from our LORD Jesus Christ very well:

1) He hates unbelief,
2) He takes faith seriously,
3) He expects you as a Christian to have faith,

4) Even satan does not respect you because of how long you have been in the church, rather satan can only respect you because of your faith in Jesus Christ.

5) The amount of the word of God you know without applying faith does not mean anything to God and satan.

6) Unbelief will frustrate your life.

7) Unbelief brings disgrace, and hinders success.

When they brought the boy to Jesus, He rebuked the devil and he departed out of him.

The disciples later came in privately and asked the Lord, why couldn't we drive out the demon?

> **Jesus answered them and said, because of your unbelief, for assuredly, I say to you, if you have faith as a mustard seed, you will say to this mountain, move from here to there, and it will move; and nothing will be impossible for you.**
> **However, this kind does not go out except by prayer and fasting**
>
> **(Matthew 17:20-21, NKJV).**

Just as Jesus told his disciples, no one receives anything from God through unbelief. It was because of their unbelief, they could not drive out the demon. However, fasting and prayer helps to build, grow and develop your faith. When you fast, pray in faith, read the word of God, and your faith will gradually build up to move mountains.

WHAT DOES FASTING MEAN?

To Ken Chukwunwejim, "Fasting is abstinence, abstinence from things that are of fundamental value or most necessary for the nourishment, entertainment or satisfaction of the body and mind. It is the way we can "go low" so that God can lift us up, give us His direction, and release His supernatural power for us and for others through us (M. and B. Chavda). Fasting is the time set aside to seek God through prayer and reading the scripture without food. Smith Wigglesworth, the greatest evangelist of the last century, once said, "but I have found prayer and fasting the greatest joy, and you will always find it so when you are led by God". In the scripture, many great men and women of God fasted and prayed. Such as Moses, David, Daniel, Ezra, Nehemiah, Jesus Christ, John the Baptist, Anna, and Paul. Fasting is recommended to every Christian because of its great importance to our Christian faith.

IMPORTANCE OF FASTING

It humbles your soul before God.

Yet when they were ill, I put on sackcloth and humbled myself with fasting (Psalm 35:13, NIV). Fasting helps you to humble yourself in repentance to God as in the case of David. The city of Nineveh fasted and humbled themselves to God in repentance of their sins. And when God saw what they did and how they turned from their evil ways, He relented and did not bring on them the destruction He had threatened (Jonah 3, NIV). Fasting comes from the humbling of one's heart in order to seek God. It helps to gain spiritual strength to soar like the Eagles in ministry, business, career and every aspects of life.

> **But they that wait upon the LORD shall renew their strength; they shall mount up with wings as eagles; they shall run, and not be weary; and they shall walk, and not faint**
>
> **(Isaiah 40:31, KJV).**

Through fasting, you control your appetites so as to give the entire time to prayer (Matthew 4:4).

Fasting helps to focus your mind completely on God to obey his command and do his will concerning your life (Acts 9:15-19, NIV).

It helps to gain spiritual power over satan, temptations, and the world (Matthew 4:1-11).

It destroys and cures unbelief (Matthew 17:20-21).

Fasting improves and boosts your faith. It is the energy medication of faith. (Matthew 17:20-21).

TYPES OF FASTING

There are four main types of fasting in the Bible.

Normal Fast

Our Lord Jesus Christ is our example. He fasted for forty days and forty nights in the wilderness to begin His earthly ministry (Matthew 4:-1-11). He ate no food and appears to have had only water according Biblical scholars. The scholars concluded that he drank water while on this fast because the bible says he was hungry, but did not say he was thirsty. Again, the devil tempted Jesus with bread, but not with water. So they assume this was a water only fast. Through this period of fasting, Jesus gained enough power over satan and temptations and was able to begin His ministry strong. Normal fasting can be extended for longer period of time while you break at intervals presumably in the evenings. Note, if you accidentally taste food while on fast, it does not mean you have broken your fast as long as you did not continue with the food. The motive behind your fast is the most important one.

FULL FAST

Some Christians can call it absolute fast or dry fast. This is the type of fasting you engage without consuming any food nor drink any liquid. Examples:

Paul's encounter with Jesus on the road to Damascus.

According to Acts 9:9, Paul fasted for three days eating neither food nor drank liquid when he encountered Jesus on the road to Damascus.

Another example is Queen Esther;

> **Then Esther sent this reply to Mordecai: 'Go, gather together all the Jews who are in Susa, and fast for me. Do not eat or drink for three days, night or day. I and my attendants will fast as you do. When this is**

done, I will go to the king, even though it is against
the law. And if I perish, I perish

(Esther 4:15-16, NIV).

This type of fasting scares demons, breaks laws and order, empowers your faith to move any mountain on your way and do mighty works. Full fast is not necessarily for three days like Saul and Esther, it can be a day or more than as the Holy Spirit leads you. The essence of fasting is not for public show like the Pharisees or some people do, the reason must be according to God's will, to seek God sincerely for the purpose acceptable unto God. Warning: please, this type of fast should be done with caution. Do not extend the recommended three days periods and break your fast with care. Avoid solid food and over eating for a while.

PARTIAL FAST

This is the type of fasting Daniel did.

At that time I, Daniel, mourned for three weeks. I
ate no choice food; no meat or wine touched my lips;
and I used no lotions at all until the three weeks
were over

(Daniel 10:2-3, NIV).

Partial fast is the type where people abstain from certain foods for a prolonged period of time. People omit meat, sweets and bread and eat only vegetables, fruits and drink water. Some people may choose to omit caffeine, or stop watching TV and give time to prayer and reading the word of God. Water is allowed on partial fast. You can do it by reducing the quality or the size of food you eat. Daniel did partial fasting for twenty one days for the will of God to come to pass on Jews in Babylon and God answered him. Partial fast will help you achieve great success in life.

SEXUAL FAST

This type requires husband and wife to agree before engaging on fasting to avoid temptation. If there is no consent, wives give your body to your husband and husbands give your body to your wives.

The husband should fulfill his marital duty to his wife, and likewise the wife to her husband. The wife does not have authority over her own body but yields it to her husband. In the same way, the husband does not have authority over his own body but yields it to his wife. Do not deprive each other except perhaps by mutual consent and for a time, so that you may devote yourselves to prayer. Then come together again so that satan will not tempt you because of your lack of self - control (1 Corinthians 7:3-5, NIV).

BEGINNING YOUR FAST

Why do you want to fast and pray? Do you want to know the will of God for your life, marriage, family, career or ministry? Do you want healing or financial breakthrough? You must have reason (s) for fasting. Write down clearly your purpose why you are fasting and depend on the Holy Spirit for guidance. Ask God for His grace to carry you through. Spend quality time to study your Bible. Surrender all your life to God to work on you. Worship and praise God with songs, hymns, psalms, or with your best way of worship. Forgive every one that offended you. Confess your sins and ask God to have mercy on you.

HOW LONG TO FAST

The duration of a Christian fast depends on the need and desire of the individual. There are no rules or regulations given on how long or often a Christian should fast. As the Holy Spirit may lead you, you can fast as long as you can. But you must be wise and allow the Holy Spirit to guide you. You can start fasting from 6am -12noon. And gradually increase it from 6am - 3pm, till you learn how to fast and pray from 6am - 6pm. From there, you can fast for days. As a beginner, please start gradually.

PHYSICAL EXPERIENCE

There are some body changes you will see as you fast. Your body will detoxify removing toxins from your system. You may feel hungry but don't eat. Be faithful to your devotion to fast. Avoid too much exercise and heavy work. Take time to rest. Avoid too much talking. Sometimes, you may encounter temptations and trouble but be rest assured that God is with you. Avoid activities that will distract your attention from God. Avoid bad companies or bad friends because you are fasting to encounter God for your needs. Pray as much as you can.

THE NEED TO FAST

The disciples of John the Baptist one day came and asked Jesus a vital question.

> **Then John's disciples came and asked Him (Jesus), 'how is it that we and the Pharisees fast often, but your disciples do not fast?**
> **Jesus answered, 'how can the guests of the bridegroom mourn while he is with them? The time will come when the bridegroom will be taken from them; then they will fast.**
>
> **(Matthew 9:14-15, NIV).**

And Jesus answered and made it clear to them,

"....can you make the friends of the bridegroom fast while he is with them?"

The answer is no. He continued and said, but the time will come when the bridegroom will be taken from them and in those days they will find the need to fast.

John's disciples had needs to fast and pray because their master was ending his ministry on earth. But the disciples of Jesus by then had no need to fast because their master Jesus was still with them. Jesus made it clear to them that the time will come when He is taken from them, His disciples will find the need to fast and pray.

IN TROUBLE TIME

In trouble times, such as war, danger, disaster, famine, judgment, worries, spiritual affliction, attacks and oppressions, fasting and prayer is needed for God to intervene.

We are living in trouble times; the world is too dangerous to live. Every day the televisions and news papers are filled with bad news of terrorism, rumours of wars, corruption, abominations, satanic oppressions, and bad news you cannot imagine to hear. It is time Christians should seek God.

Mr Mordecai told Esther, 'For if you remain silent at this time, relief and deliverance for the Jews will arise from another place, but you and your Father's family will perish'.

If Christian remains silent at this time, watching Islamic terrorists, they will destroy and take over the world. And remember, nobody is saved. They are waging Jihad war which means conversion to Islam by force. Christians, it is time to arise and pull down this strong hold of Islamic terrorism nick named Isis, through the power of fasting and prayer.

When Mordecai learned of all that had been done, he tore his clothes, Put on sackcloth and ashes, and went out into the city, wailing loudly and bitterly. But he went only as far as the king's gate, because no one clothed in sackcloth was allowed to enter it.

In every province to which the edict and the order of the king came, there was great mourning among the Jews, with fasting, weeping and wailing. Many lay in sackcloth and ashes. When Esther's eunuchs and female attendants came and told her about Mordecai, she was in great distress. She sent clothes for him to put on instead of his sackcloth, but he would not accept them.

Then Esther summoned Hathak, one of the King's eunuchs assigned to attend her, and ordered him to find out what is troubling Mordecai and why? So Hathak went out to Mordecai in the open square of the city in front of the king's gate. Mordecai told him everything that had happened to him, including the exact amount of money Haman had promised to pay into the royal treasury for the destruction of the Jews. He also gave him a copy of the text of the edict for their annihilation, which had been published in Susa, to show to Esther and explain it to her, and he told him to instruct her to go into the king's presence to beg for mercy and plead with him for her people.

Hathak went back and reported to Esther what Mordecai had said. Then she instructed him to say to Mordecai, 'All the king's officials and the people of the royal provinces know that for any man or woman who approaches the king in the inner court without being summoned the king has but one law: that they be put to death unless the king extends the gold sceptre to them and spares their lives. But thirty days have passed since I was called to go to the king'. When Esther's words were reported to Mordecai, he sent back this answer:

> 'Do not think that because you are in the king's house you alone of all the Jews will escape. For if you remain silent at this time, relief and deliverance for

the Jews will arise from another place, but you and your father's family will perish. And who knows but that you have come to your royal position for such a time as this?'

Then Esther sent this reply to Mordecai:

'Go, gather together all the Jews who are in Susa, and fast for me. Do not eat or drink for three days, night or day. I and my attendants will fast as you do. When this is done, I will go to the king, even though it is against the law. And if I perish, I perish

(Esther 4, NIV).

Haman the enemy of the Jews paid ten thousand talents of silver to the king's treasury to annihilate all the Jews - Young and old, men, women, children on a single day.

When Mordecai heard the bad news, he tore his clothes, put on sackcloth and ashes, and went out into the city, wailing loudly and bitterly. He went straight to the entrance of the king's gate to make his voice heard to Queen Esther.

The bad news of Islamic terrorist has reached the whole world. There is nobody even children that have not heard about the atrocity of this evil group called Islamic terrorist. They are spreading from country to country, city to city, killing and been killed. These evil groups are attacking churches, shopping centers, schools and cinemas, destroying our cultures and values with the single purpose to force everybody in the world to convert to Islam. God forbid.

For how long should Christians remain silent? People are afraid of going on holiday or to events because of this evil group. How long should we Christians remain silent?

These evil groups are well sponsored just like Haman paid heavily to annihilate the Jews. Their aim is to completely annihilate Christianity in the world. For example, remember what they are doing in Iraq, Syria, Northern Nigeria, Somalia, Pakistan, Afghanistan, Egypt and France.

Immediately, Mordecai heard about the evil Haman planned against Jews, he tore his clothes, put on sackcloth and ashes, and went out into the city, wailing loudly and bitterly with fasting, and went straight to the king's gate to report to queen Esther. This is a Holy anger. Christians should be angry of what is happening in the world today and come out of their comfort zones and seek for God's intervention for the peace of the world.

On 26ᵗʰ July, 2016 by 9am, a Catholic priest was murdered during church mass service. The evil terrorists besieged the church in Normandy France, and slaughtered the throat of the priest and injured some many worshippers in the church in a European country. For how long should we Christians remain silent?

> **Mordecai warned Esther: Do not think that because you are in the king's house you alone of all the Jews will escape. For if you remain silent at this time, relief and deliverance for the Jews will arise from another place, but you and your Father family will perish**
> **(Esther 4:13-14,NIV).**

Do not think that because you are in Britain, America, Canada, Australia, China, South Africa, Singapore and other Christian majority nations that you are safe from the Islamic terrorism. If Christians remain silent relying on military and arms, this evil organization may destroy Christianity and the world. No place, city or country is saved in this world now. Who knows who is next and which country is next for them to attack? It is time to stand up, fast and pray to root out and pull down these evil groups.

> **Then Esther sent this reply to Mordecai: 'Go, gather together all the Jews who are in Susa, and fast for me. Do not eat or drink for three days, night or day. I and my attendants will fast as you do. When this is done, I will go to the king, even though it is against the law. And if I perish, I perish**
> **(Esther 4:15-16, NIV).**

Christians, let us not remain silent watching these evil monsters called Islamic terrorist destroy us. Motivate, encourage and gather together men and women of God in your local area to fast and pray to demolish the strongholds of this evil organization called Islamic state.

The prayer of a righteous person is powerful and effective

(James 5:16b, NIV).

Christians, our prayers are very effective and powerful to destroy and pull down any strongholds. Therefore, your prayers can do more powerful work than arms and ammunitions because they have God's power to pull down strongholds.

The weapons we fight with are not the weapons of the world. On the contrary, they have divine power to demolish strongholds

(2 Corinthian 10:4, NIV).

THE CURE OF UNBELIEF

Mountains of life do not respect you because you call yourself Christians. They don't care how long you have been in the church. Maybe, you have been in the church for ten years, or fifty years, they can only respect and obey you because of your faith in Jesus Christ. The disciples of Jesus could not heal the boy because of their unbelief. They were humiliated, disgraced and confused because of lack of faith.

> **Then the disciples came to Jesus privately and said, "Why could we not cast it out?" So Jesus said to them, "Because of your unbelief; for assuredly, I say to you, if you have faith as a mustard seed, you will say to this mountain, 'move from here to there,' and it will move; and nothing will be impossible for you. However, this kind does not go out except by prayer and fasting."**
>
> **(Matthew 17:19 - 21, NKJV)**

Unbelief will disgrace, humiliate and stop people from reaching their potentials in life. It delays, hinders, and destroys wonderful visions and careers. Life looks hard when people cannot believe God. People are asking too many questions today about God and His works due to unbelief. God exists and His works are true and real, but satan has covered the heart of some individuals so that they will find it hard to believe God. Unbelief stops people from receiving answers to their prayer.

> **But when you ask, you must believe and not doubt, because the one who doubts is like a wave of the sea,**

blown and tossed by the wind, that person should not expect to receive anything from the Lord

(James 1:6-7, NIV).

Unbelief is a great obstacle in life, and so negative that it will always say there is a casting down. Unbelief separates people from God, (Hebrew 3:12). It keeps people away from purity, righteousness and the grace of God. It does not allow his captives to believe and seek the free help of God. Unbelief makes people unstable in all their ways.

JESUS, HELP ME OVERCOME MY UNBELIEF

Prayer and fasting with the word of God destroys and cures unbelief. They energize and boost your faith. **However, this kind does not go out except by prayer and fasting (Matthew 17:21, NKJV).** If anyone is lacking faith, fasting and prayer will improve and make your faith strong to overcome mountains in your way. Even the sick boy's father was lacking faith after Jesus rebuked him he cried out and ask Jesus for help.

Immediately the boy's father exclaimed, "I do believe; help me overcome my unbelief"

(Mark 9:24, NIV).

Jesus wants to help you overcome your unbelief. Cry out to Him now. As much as it is possible fast and pray and ask Jesus to help you overcome your unbelief just as the boy's father did. Ask Him to give you the spirit of faith to believe the word and the power of God so that you can live a faithful and fruitful Christian life.

> **Truly I tell you, if you have faith as small as a mustard seed, you can say to this mountain, "Move from here to there," and it will move. Nothing will be impossible for you**
>
> **(Matthew 17:20, NIV).**

BEGINNING A NEW CALLING, CAREER OR PROJECT.

Fasting and prayer help to draw your spirit closer to know the plan of God concerning your life.

> **While they were worshipping the LORD and fasting, the Holy Spirit said, 'set apart for me Barnabas and Saul for the work to which I have called them. So after they had fasted and prayed, they placed their hands on them and sent them off**
>
> **(Acts 13:2-3, NIV).**

While the disciples were worshipping the Lord and fasting, the Holy Spirit said, 'set apart for me Barnabas and Saul for the work to which I have called them. Through Fasting and prayer the Holy Spirit will make the calling of God in your life clear. He will show you what God want you to do, how to achieve it and where to achieve it. It is through fasting and prayer Barnabas and Saul understood the plan of God concerning them. The disciples placed their hands on them, prayed and sent them to do the work. There is a work or plan God has for your life.

The book of Jeremiah 29:11, NIV, says,

For I know the plans I have for you, 'declares the LORD, 'plans to prosper you and not to harm you, 'plans to give hope and a future'.

When I was in the university, one Sunday afternoon I went to a scripture Union campus fellowship meeting. After the fellowship meeting, the fellowship president came to greet me. As we were sharing greetings, he gave me a wrapped piece of paper, because every where was busy after the fellowship, I pocketed the gift and did not think to open it. When I got home, I dropped my bible and other items with me on the table. Dipped my hand in my pocket and brought out the gift. As I was about to open it, I heard the Holy Spirit speak to me very loud and said, **'I have a plan for you'.**

When I opened the piece of paper and saw what was written there was Jeremiah 29:11. I was trembled and thought deeply. I told my mate in the room what had happened. He agreed with me that after our final Architectural degree presentations, which were just few weeks from then, we would go to scripture Union camp of Faith, Okigwe, Nigeria, and seek the face of God for four days concerning His plans for our lives.

On the second day of the four days fasting and prayer in the camp, as we were going to pray that early morning, my friend said to me can we have some discussion before proceeding to prayers? I answered yes of course. When we sat down, he asked me, did you have a plan of travelling abroad? I replied, why did you ask? Then he shared the dream he had last night to me. He said the Lord came to him in the dream and said, **'very soon this friend will take the gospel back to the people that brought it to us'**. Then he asked me again do you have plans of travelling abroad? I answered yes. This happened in November, 2006, in scripture Union Nigeria camp of Faith, Okigwe, Nigeria.

See brethren, fasting and prayer unveils the plans of God to light so that you can clearly see and understand them well.

Whenever you propose to take any major step in life, it is important to effectively seek God to understand his plans and purpose for your life especially through fasting and Prayer.

Jesus Christ before He began his earthly ministry went into the wilderness for forty days and forty nights to fast and pray. Through fasting and prayer, He gained power over satan, temptations and human oppositions (Matthew 4:1-11).

It is good to first seek God first before you begin your career or project through fasting and prayer so that He will establish your plans and show you which path to take.

> **Seek His will in all you do, and He will show you which path to take.**
>
> **(Proverbs 3:6, NLT).**

> **Commit to the LORD whatever you do, and He will establish your plans.**
>
> **(Proverbs 16:3, NIV).**

DIVINE BREAKTHROUGH AND HELP

When Nehemiah heard about the bad situations of the Jewish remnant that survived the exile, the wall of Jerusalem broken down and its gates burned down with fire, he was broken in the spirit and wept. He fasted and prayed before God to grant him favour before the king to give him permission to go and rebuild the wall of Jerusalem.

In the month of Kislev in the twentieth year, while I was in the citadel of Susa, Hanani, one of my brothers, came from Judah with some other men, and I questioned them about the Jewish remnant that had survived the exile, and also about Jerusalem.

They said to me, 'those who survived the exile and are back in the province are in great trouble and disgrace. The wall of Jerusalem is broken down, and its gates have burned with fire'.

When I heard these things, I sat down and wept. For some days I mourned and fasted and prayed before the God of heaven.

Then I said: 'LORD, the God of heaven, the great and awesome God, who keeps his covenant of love with those who love Him and keep His commandments, let your ear be attentive and your eyes open to hear the prayer your servant is praying before you day and night for your servants, the people of Israel. I confess the sins we Israelites, including myself and my Father's family, have committed against you. We have acted very wickedly towards you. We have not obeyed the commands, decrees and laws you gave your servant Moses. Remember the instruction you gave your servant Moses, saying, "If you are unfaithful, I will scatter you among the nations, but if you return to me and obey my commands, then even if your exiled people are at the farthest horizon, I will gather them from

there and bring them to the place I have chosen as a dwelling for my name".

'They are your servants and your people, whom you redeemed by your great strength, and your mighty hand. Lord, let your ear be attentive to the prayer of this your servant and to the prayer of your servants who delight in revering your name. Give your servant success today by granting him favour in the presence of this man'. (Nehemiah 1:1-11, NIV)

Nehemiah began his prayers by praising, revering and exalting God for his faithfulness in keeping his covenants to those who love Him and keep His commandments. He confessed his sins, the sins of his father's family and the national sins of Israel. That is a sign of humility before God. He continued by reminding God about His word and promises to his people. He concluded by asking God to give him success by granting him favour before the king for permission to go and rebuild the wall of Jerusalem.

No matter what is your need, when you come before God, understand who He is.

Our God is the God of heaven and earth, our father in heaven, the Almighty,

Jehovah (I AM means the one who is, the self - Existent one),

Jehovah - Rapha (The Lord who heals),

Jehovah - Rohi (The Lord is my Shepherd),

Jehovah - Tsidkenu (The Lord our righteousness),

Immanuel (God is with us),

El Shaddai (The All sufficient one),

El Roi (The God who sees me),

Elohim (The All-Powerful one, creator),

Adonai, (My great LORD).

Put on humility like Nehemiah and confess your sins and ask Him for mercy over your life. Nehemiah also knew the secret of receiving answers from God by praying with the word of God and reminding Him about His promises. When you remind God what His word says concerning your need He will act quickly. Praying with the word of God and reminding Him about His promises holds God accountable to answer you speedily.

In fasting and praying for breakthrough or divine help, pray with the word of God and remind Him about His promises and you will see He will answer you speedily.

He continued in Chapter 2;

In the month of Nisan in the twentieth year of king Artaxerxes, when wine was brought for him, I took the wine and gave it to the

king. I had not been sad in his presence before, so the king asked me, 'why does your face look so sad when you are not ill? This can be nothing but sadness of heart'. I was very much afraid, but I said to the king, 'may the king live forever! Why should my face not look sad when the city where my ancestors are buried lies in ruins, and its gates have been destroyed by fire?

The king said to me, 'what is it you want?' Then I prayed to the God of heaven, and I answered the king, 'If it pleases the king and if your servant has found favour in his sight, let him send me to the city in Judah where my ancestors are buried so that I can rebuild it? Then the king, with the queen sitting beside him, asked me, 'How long will your journey take, and when will you get back? It pleased the king to send me; so I set a time. I also said to him, 'if it pleases the king, may I have letters to the governors of Tranns - Euphrates, so that they will provide me safe - conduct until I arrive in Judah? And may I have a letter to Asaph, keeper of the royal park, so he will give timber to make beams for the gates of the citadel by the temple and for the city wall and for the residence I will occupy? And because the gracious hand of my God was on me, the king granted my requests, (Nehemiah 2:1-8, NIV).

The favour of God is unlimited for breakthrough or divine help, God places His gracious hand upon us so that whatever we ask will be granted. It means uncommon favour, like Nehemiah, therefore, if we ask God anything in faith, it will be given to us.

Fasting and prayer break barriers, protocols and opens doors for breakthroughs and help. How can a slave like Nehemiah go before the king? It was only possible through the force of fasting and prayer.

When Nehemiah saw that God has given him favour before the king, he asked for more things. He requested for more things than he planned. And because the gracious hand of God was on him, the king had no option but to grant him all his requests.

Brethren, it is a divine opportunity to come before God in fasting and prayer. The favour of God is more than the volume of water in the sea. Ask God as many things as possible because His gracious hand is on you and the windows of heaven are open unto you, all your requests will be granted to you. Fasting and prayer is a divine spiritual force that opens the iron doors that look impossible and give you access to your breakthroughs.

After Esther and the rest of the Jews fasted and prayed for three days and nights, Queen Esther went to see the king without invitation, to plead for the salvation of the Jews. According to the law, any person who approaches the king in the inner court without being summoned by the king, the king has but one law, that person must be put to death unless the king extends the gold scepter to them and spares their lives. As all the Jews in Susa were fasting and praying, Esther boldly went to the king. When the king saw Her, He was pleased at her and spared her life because the gracious hand of God was upon Queen Esther (Esther 4). In difficult situations, fasting and prayer help to make the impossible possible. It grants us a divine access, success and favour to whatsoever thing we are in need of, because the gracious hand of God is on us. Fasting and prayer will turn everything around to our own good. There is nothing impossible with God. Seek God through fasting and prayer for any hard situation in your life. And He will grant you success and favour today in Jesus name.

CHAPTER 5

Conclusion

There is no Christian that can do without prayer. Just as water is a basic necessity for life, prayer is a necessity for healthy Christian living. It is a fellowship, relationship and communication between man and God. Let us therefore return to the school of prayer with strong desire and hunger, and ask our master Jesus Christ, "teach us how to pray like Him".

When we come to pray, let us always remember that we are in the presence of God and He is with us. God knows our needs even before we starts to pray. Therefore, ask in faith and it will be given to us. It is only the name of Jesus Christ God authorizes us to pray. Allow the Holy Spirit to guide you and pray with the word of God. The posture of prayer can be kneeling, sitting, standing, bowing, and lying down, lifting hands and eyes towards heaven.

Our Lord Jesus Christ introduced God to us as our Father in heaven. Even Paul the apostle referred God as our Father in heaven. When we come to pray, let us know that it is a time of a lovely relationship with our heavenly Father, to express our friendship and desires together. Do not forget to worship to Him appropriate to His glory. Think of what He can do, and how He delights to hear our prayers. And be confident that whatever we ask according to His will, will be given to us. Avoid pride, put on humility and confess your sins to God. Forgive those that sinned against you, so that God will also forgive our sins. God demands thanksgiving. Give Him thanks properly for what He has done because it is what He requires for His kindness shown to us. Remember, even till today, believers all over the world, are still doing mighty things and obtaining great results through prayer. "Elijah was a human being, even as we are. He prayed earnestly that it would not rain, and it did not rain on the land for three and a half years. Again he prayed, and the heavens gave rain, and the earth produced its crops" (James 5:17-18, NIV).

There are things that hinder our prayers such as unforgiveness, sin, satan, wrong motives, disunity, doubt, worries, pride, and laziness.

Forgiveness is one of the conditions of answered prayer. If we forgive other people when they sin against us, our heaven Father will also forgive us. But if we do not forgive others their sins, our Father in heaven will not forgive us our sins, and our prayers will not be answered. Forgiveness brings purity and draws us closer to God but unforgiveness separates us from Him. It is necessary that we forgive in order to release us from the agony of bondage and be free. It helps to progress and be productive in life. Forgiveness is good for our health. It brings healing to broken relationships, reduces stress, worries, blood pressure, depression, and hostility. It leads to stronger immune system, improved healthier heart and increases self esteem. Begin now to forgive others their sins like Joseph, our Lord Jesus Christ, Stephen, Nelson Mandela and other great men.

Prayer and fasting is a powerful weapon believers uses to demolish satanic strong holds, evil thoughts, unbelief and overcome human oppositions. It is a means we can go low so that God can lift us up, give us His direction and release His supernatural power for us and for others through us. There are types of fasting such as normal fast, full fast, partial fast, and sexual fast.

Prayer and fasting is necessary in times of war, danger, disaster, famine, judgment, worries, spiritual afflictions and oppressions. It is the right medicine for unbelief and doubt. Prayer and fasting helps to gain direction in the beginning of new calling, career and any type of project. It is important to effectively seek God especially when you propose to take any major step in life. It helps to open impossible doors for us so that God will grant us favour and success in whatsoever is our needs. Prayer and fasting will turn everything around to your own favour. God will give us success in anything we seek from Him according to His will, through fasting and prayer.

References

CHAPTER 1

Andrew Murray, Lord teach us to pray, by Revival press, 2016, page 4.

Bruce McLennan, Mary Slessor (A life on the altar for God). By Christian focus publications Ltd, 2014, pg 163.

Charles Spurgeon, Sermons on prayer, published by Christian classics treasury on 20th April, 2012.

Gbile Akanni, Quest for God, by Peace house publications, 2007, pages 84-90, 96 -99.

Kenneth E. Hagin, The Triumphant church by Faith Library publications, 1993, pp. 157 – 158.

Roberts Liardon, God's Generals by Whitaker House and Tulsa Ok, 1996, pp. 211.

Smith Wigglesworth, Greater works – Experiencing God's power by Whitaker House, 2000, pages 221-224.

Smith Wigglesworth, The power of Faith by Whitaker House, 2000, pages 384 – 389.

CHAPTER 2

Kenneth E. Hagin, Five Hindrances to Growth in Grace by RHMA Bible church, 1980, pages 19-21.

Sam Wellman, Mary Slessor – Queen of Calabar by Barbour publishing, INC., 1918, page 91.

CHAPTER 3

Gail L., Rick S., Dale I., Elizabeth B., Heidemarie K., Journal of Behavioral medicine, by Springer Publishing Int'l AG, December 2011, volume 34, Issue 6, pp. 414 – 425.

Neil T. Anderson, The Bondage Breaker, by Monarch Books, 2007, pp. 225 – 230.

Nelson R. Mandela, Long Walk to Freedom by Abacus, 1995, pp 679 – 745.

Richard Attenborough, The words of Gandhi, by Newmarket press, 1996, pp. 66 – 71.

Printed in the United States
By Bookmasters